Joe Addison

The Weir House,
Alresford.

BID THE WORLD GOOD-NIGHT

Bid the world good-night

A symposium
edited and
produced by
Ralph Ricketts

Search Press . London

First published in 1981 by Search Press Ltd., 2/10 Jerdan Place,
London SW6 5PT, in Britain, Ireland and associated territories.

ISBN 0 85532 446 5

Phototypeset by Input Typesetting Ltd, London SW19 8DR
Printed and bound in Great Britain at The Camelot Press Ltd,
Southampton, for Search Press Ltd, 2/10 Jerdan Place, London SW6 5PT

Only a little more
I have to write,
Then I'll give o'er,
and bid the world good-night.
                    Robert Herrick (1591–1674)

Do not let me hear
Of the wisdom of old men, but rather of their folly
Their fear of fear and frenzy, their fear of possession,
Of belonging to another, or to others, or to God.
. . .
Old men ought to be explorers.
                    T. S. Eliot (1888–1965)

L'homme a l'âge des sentiments qu'il éprouve, et la
femme celui des sentiments qu'elle inspire.
                    Private Diaries of the Rt Hon. Sir Algernon
                    West, GCB, ed. Horace Hutchinson
                    (London, 1922)

I know I probably have the advantage of you, of most people.
I have conquered the fear of death . . . I have been to the top
of the mountain and have seen the Promised Land.
                    Martin Luther King

Acknowledgments

Grateful acknowledgment is made to the following publishers for the use of copyright material: Chatto & Windus; Enitharmon Press; Harvill Press; Hodder & Stoughton; John Murray.

Where it seemed relevant, I asked contributors to let me know how old they were. Since there has been a delay between collection and publication these ages are slightly out-of-date. I have decided to leave them as they were when the contributions were written. Meanwhile, the young novelist, Dominic Cooper, has won the Somerset Maugham award.

Contents

	Page
Introduction by Ralph Ricketts	1
Towards the twilight of life	4
Contributions from:	
Joseph Addison	6
Lady Askwith	9
Paul Beard	13
Sir Lennox Berkeley	19
Sir John Betjeman	22
Douglas Brown	24
Rev. Anthony Bullen	26
Rt Rev. B. C. Butler	29
Lord David Cecil	32
Zoë Comper	36
Dominic Cooper	37
Martin Cooper	42
Georgina Denison	44
William Douglas Home	47
Dame Daphne du Maurier	48
S. I. Goldsmith	54
Sir Paul Grey	55
Harman Grisewood	60
D. J. Hall	64
Manya Harari	69
L. P. Hartley	73
Rosemary Haughton	76
Rt Rev. Trevor Huddleston	81
Michael James Laws	85
The Earl of Longford	87
General Sir James Marshall-Cornwall	92

Catherine Marshall	95
Sir Frederick Mason	96
Madeleine Masson	98
Rt Hon. Lord Maybray-King	99
Paul Maze	105
Yehudi Menuhin	106
Dr Neil Micklem	107
Naomi Mitchison	111
Patrick O'Donovan	115
Dame Iris Origo	118
Ruth Pitter	121
Brigadier, Lord Porritt	129
Kathleen Raine	134
Dr Peter Riley	143
Vera Bloodgood Scribner	149
John Sparrow	150
Robert Speaight	151
Dame Freya Stark	156
Rt Hon. Sir John Stephenson	163
Lady Stocks	169
Rt Rev. Mervyn Stockwood	170
'Harold Sutton'	179
Philip Toynbee	184
Sir George Trevelyan, Bart	188
Margaret Trouncer	198
Harry Walden	200
Dom Alberic Stacpoole	202
Epilogue by Ralph Ricketts	207

Introduction

Ralph Ricketts

Numerous books and articles are written nowadays about babyhood, before and after birth – not to mention abortion; about childhood, about teenagehood, if one may coin such a word, but comparatively few about old age and death. We have become prudish about old age and death, as prudish as our grandparents were about sex. We call an old man or woman elderly, a senior citizen; we do not die, we pass on, or away. It is difficult to believe that, not so very long ago, old age was not only readily admitted but old people were revered, even feared. Now it appears to be taken for granted that we are interested in, and should be instructed in, only the first half of life. This, I think, is a misconception. I believe people are interested in death, if only at certain moments – when, for instance, it strikes a member of the family or a close friend. It is true, that when we are young our own old age and death are inconceivable. Other people may grow old and die but not we. As we grow older our perspective changes. Old age and death creep forward out of the darkness of the inconceivable and stare us in the face. For a time, we may shut our eyes in the hope that if we refuse to return their gaze these twin jackals will slink back into the shadows out of which they crept. It doesn't work. In the end, we have to come to terms with them.

The scarcity of books about old age and death gave me the idea of inviting contributions on the subject from well-known men and women of various ages and professions, with a view to a symposium, the profits from which would go to *Help the Aged*. I aimed to make the collection representative of as many points of view as possible. To my regret, the avowed agnostics and atheists whom I approached, with one shining exception who lives in the same village and therefore could not escape me, either did not reply or declined to contribute. I can understand that to an atheist death might qualify as a 'non-subject', *le néant*, but not, surely, old age which is visible, even tangible every day. From others, the response has been magnificent. I would like to express my warm gratitude to the men and women many, if not all, extremely busy, who, by their personal contributions have made this collection possible, also to those who have allowed me to quote from their published works.

Not long ago, I listened to a programme on the wireless in which several distinguished doctors described the establishment of a unit to 'screen' old people (it appears that at first the general practitioners in the district opposed the scheme but later came round to it). We have ante-natal clinics which tell a prospective mother how to prepare for the arrival of her baby, baby clinics which tell her how to look after it when it has arrived; marriage-guidance clinics abound but, so far as I know, there are few, if any, specialized clinics to which old men and women can take their problems – social, physical, mental and spiritual. Old age has been described by Lord Hugh Cecil as 'the out-patients' department of Purgatory'. Perhaps we should learn in advance how to comport ourselves as out-patients, even how to enter Purgatory. I have read that common reactions in a patient told he is about to die are first disbelief, then anger and depression, and only later acceptance. This would appear to suggest that some sort of preparation might be helpful. It is said that a former headmaster of a famous Roman Catholic public school, when told by the headmaster of an even more famous Anglican public school with, one suspects, slight asperity, 'We educate our boys for life', retorted, 'And we educate our boys for death'. This may have been an over-reaction but it contains a neglected truth.

On the whole, the picture of old age and death which emerges from these contributions is consoling, even inspiring. Many of the contributors express a tranquil acceptance, not only of death but of old age which, perhaps, is more remarkable in the light of what one contributor writes, quoting *Amiel's Journal*: 'To grow old is more difficult than to die. To know how to grow old is the master work of wisdom'. A number of contributors appear to accept the probability, if not the certainty of another life; a few regard joy as proper to old age, one pointing out 'how, in fact, the blessing of God himself is seen to consist in length of days. The patriarchs of The Old Testament, "the friends of God", Abraham, Isaac, Joseph are all represented as "of good old age . . . full of years" '. Dietrich Bonhoeffer spoke of death as 'the supreme festival on the road to freedom'. One contributor makes a witty comparison between death and birth. She writes: 'The ordeal of birth looms over them (the unborn) as the prospect of death looms over us. Birth itself must be a shock for the infant . . . the rage and grief expressed in the noises young infants make . . . make me just as ready to say "Poor old baby!" as I am to say "Poor old soul!" at the sight of a miserable old man or woman'.

How best to cope with old age and death must remain, to a large extent, a matter of temperament. What would suit one old man or woman might not suit another. Each reader will naturally look among these contributions for the aspect and approach which most appeals to himself. He will find represented here commonsense, joy, acceptance, faith, hope and humour.

Towards the twilight of life

ad Deum qui laetificat juventutem meum

Youth, the age of dark hair, is swiftly gone.
In the time of your youth, forget not your Maker.
While ill days are far off yet, before the years draw near
Of which you will say: 'I like them not'.

Forget not your Maker in the time of your Youth,
While the sun and its light, and the moon and its stars
                                    are not darkened,
Before the clouds are yet gathered, the clouds that
                                    bring rain.

For one day, door-keepers will tremble and guardians
                                    be bowed,
Women shall cease to grind at the mill,
As they and the day grow dark at their windows
And their door to the street remains shut.

One day shall the mill grinding slacken
And the song of the bird shall be stilled,
As all sound of singing is silenced.
Then shall hills be a burden and the highway a cause
                                    for dread.

Still shall the almond tree blossom,
The grasshopper surfeit with food,
Still shall the caper-berry scatter its fruit,
Though man is drawing near his last home.

Already mourners are afoot in the streets
Even before the silver cord has snapped
Or the golden lamp has been broken,
Before the pitcher at the fountain is shattered,
Before the pulley at the wall is cracked.

Already mourners are astir in public
Before the dust returns to the earth it came from
And the spirit to God who gave it.
Forget not your Maker in this hour of your youth.

Ecclesiastes XII: interpretation by Dom Alberic J. Stacpoole,
OSB

Joseph Addison

Retired oil executive and farmer.

How fortunate are those whose religious beliefs bring to them the certainty, or near certainty, of a life after death, a reunion with loved ones and a continuing happy existence where, in the words of the hymn-writer, 'pleasures banish pain'. These beliefs, if sincerely held, are clearly the best recipe for approaching old age and death in a defiant and even exuberant frame of mind which must make (and indeed has made, in the case of the noble army of martyrs in the past) the pains of approaching dissolution and the pangs of death so much easier to bear.

But for many of us, try as we may, the dogmas of the Christian religion are hard to accommodate within the bounds of our very logic-bound minds and we are cast back onto a more general feeling that, when we consider all the beauty, intricacy and scientific wonder of the universe, there must lie somewhere behind it all a purpose, a Creator. What sort of a Creator? We have been brought up as Christians to believe that God the Father, who in the beginning created heaven and earth and all that therein is, was and is omnipotent and omniscient. He therefore knew when he embarked on his great experiment what it would entail in terms of joy, of suffering, of failure, of success; and *prima facie* it seems fair to lay at his door the responsibility for famine, tempest, drought, sickness and suffering of every description. But no, it is said, there was what the lawyers would call a *novus actus interveniens* – a new occurrence – namely the fall of man and

6

the exercise of his own free-will in ways which thwart the beneficent design of the Creator.

Very well, let us side-step this issue. I have been a countryman all my life and I am fascinated and enthralled by the marvellous intricacies of nature. I have also been a farmer and have some acquaintance with the diseases to which animals and birds are prone. And having observed the slow, sickening, agonising deaths which in nature come to so many creatures, whether from wounds received from their natural enemies or from illness of every description, or from starvation; and having pondered the cycle of the common lung-worm in cattle and considered the apparent uselessness of this parasite (among a host of others) and the amount of pain and suffering that it causes; indeed, having reflected that the whole of nature involves suffering of many kinds and that there has, so far as I am aware, never been any suggestion that this is due to the exercise of free-will by animals, thereby thwarting the beneficent design of the Creator – I find myself driven away from the concept of a Creator who is at once beneficent, omnipotent and omniscient. For if he could see when he embarked on the creation of nature (let us leave out man for the moment or we will be back in the free-will argument) exactly where this would lead to in terms of pain and suffering, then I am bound to doubt his beneficence; and if he would not see this then I am bound to doubt his omniscience and indeed his wisdom in embarking on such a project at all.

It will, I know, be argued that this type of observation and reasoning is the product of a finite mind, necessarily limited in its horizons, and that a finite mind is not a good weapon with which to probe the infinite. In reply to which I can only plead that it is the mind which the Creator vouchsafed to me and the only weapon that I have to hand. Beyond this there is faith, by which we mean that when reason stops and there is a gap to be filled – and a gap which is by far the most fundamental consideration that will ever come our way – we should abandon all that we have ever been taught about a rational approach to a problem and jump to a conclusion which suits us.

As I said at the beginning, how fortunate are those who are able sincerely to do this. And we agnostics are left without comfort, hoping against hope that if indeed there turns out to be a Judgment Day the Creator will deal kindly with us; recognising that it was he who fitted us up with a finite mind incapable of grasping infinity. Perhaps he might feel that those of us who find the final step of faith too big to take should at least receive credit for having hoed our row in life as straight as we knew how. But then again, perhaps this is just wishful thinking.

Lady Askwith

Daughter of the late Archibald Peel. Widow of first and last Baron Askwith. Contributed by her daughter, Betty Askwith, novelist and biographer.

We fall on guard, and, after all,
it is but a friend that comes to meet us.

(Stevenson)

Very few people, except Stevenson, have ever found a good word to say for old age. They apologise for it, they disfigure it, they pretend it isn't there, they are ashamed of it. There are many who, when in the company of younger people, seem afraid to be themselves – they either pretend they too are, as Louis XIV's courtier said, 'De l'âge de tout le monde', or they seem inclined to apologise for still being in the world at all.

There are, of course, many varieties of old age: the old age of childhood, which is a tiresome one and the cause of many snubs to those, especially, who have been spoilt and are growing out of their infant charms; the old age of first youth, which often seems older than anyone could really be, and more desponding. Then the old age, which is really middle age, of those who are 'still young' – what Rudyard Kipling calls 'the turn into the straight' – that most difficult time of life, when the hair begins to turn grey and every day seems to deepen the lines in the face. One tries to cope with it by using remedies, and endeavours to persuade oneself that it is, and looks, still the same really; and one can't.

And, finally, there is the best of them all – old age itself, real true old age, the summing-up of one's life here below.

9

Every portion of existence has its own gifts and capabilities and charm, and I venture to say that those which old age brings are not the least or the worst of them, if we look at them aright. Roughly, I should call them freedom and peace. It is time to unload – 'Unarm, Eros, the long day's task is done', and if we are granted a quiet space, with some of our loved ones left, free from real pain or deprivation of any sense, it should be, perhaps, one of the happiest times of our lives.

For look how the troubles and worries of life fall away from us then. How we struggled to get on – if ambitious, to work for our children; to make and keep a place in life; with some to excel in their profession; with others to grow rich; with others, again, to stand out of the particular ruck in which they were born; with many to make a living at all. As we got older, we wondered if we had really done all we could, if the right way had been taken; if we could even keep on the hillock to which we had attained with so much labour.

Even the little things of life, for a woman – how much care and energy they needed. To keep the house nice, the food good, the servants happy, to dress becomingly without spending too much, to keep hair, complexion, nails, etc., at their best, to do all that should be done in the little tiny things which make up so much of a woman's lot in life – how tiring it sometimes was. And now, one by one the shackles fall away. In life, one's own life, one has done the most that could be done; there is no use in struggling any more. For our children we have done our best, and must leave it at that. For one's own little personal worries it is of no use to bother any longer; one's appearance, provided it passes in a crowd, doesn't matter; one's friends are made, one's routine is complete. It is perhaps possible to see more clearly the real values of things we have tried for. If they were false we leave them with a smile; if true we pass them on to younger and perhaps abler hands.

The great gift of freedom has been granted. And with freedom should come peace. The time for great effort is over.

We could not, even if we tried, keep abreast with the newer ways, the different appreciations, really understand and enter into the young manner of regarding life. It may be right, it may be wrong; it is probably partly both, but it is not ours. But should we therefore sit down and say that we can no longer help the great causes, that we are of no use in the world and can only eat the bread of idleness? Never!

The old should have found freedom – that is not for the young; they are in harness and must do their bit. But what of the other great gift, peace? I had the good fortune to marry one whose mission it was to make peace, and it taught me the value of it, and the little, little things that turn peace into strife – the want of understanding that makes enemies of those who should be friends, the tragedy when they cannot be brought together. 'The beginning of strife', said the wisest man on earth, 'is as the letting out of water'.

Here the old can, and should, help. If one reads the Bible carefully one notices the difference of rewards as promised in the Old and New Testaments. In the Old Testament it was riches and honour and glory, wives and possessions and material good. In the New Testament there is little promised, only two things – knowledge and peace. True, they mean all the world. Surely, if one can attain peace in one's old age, and can help to spread it, one is doing the last best work of all. I don't mean the peace imaged by those pacifists described by the poet as 'fighting like devils for conciliation, hating each other for the love of God', but the inward peace, the peace that passeth understanding, which, when we have it ourselves, we can help to spread.

If we can no longer carry the stones for the builders of the temple on which we have set our hearts, we can bring the mortar which binds them together.

We can, if we have discovered anything of the secrets of life – the secrets we used to have no time to unravel – bring people together, help them to see that often they are trying for the same thing under different names; that bitterness, ill-temper, and hatred and malice are foolish, passing things, and that the real end is peace. And for ourselves – not to pretend any more, not to struggle and fret any more, just to be ourselves and help where we can.

Is that old age? If so, then what a friend indeed has come to meet us!

Paul Beard

President of the College of Psychic Studies, and a member of the Society for Psychical Research.

My concern with death, extending over many years, in fact almost from young manhood, has been a rather specialised one: it is with death as a bridge. Evidence has shown that it is possible for many to return over this bridge and convey their present feelings and thoughts to those of us still on the near side. Therefore death has long ceased to be fearful, though still awesome and mysterious: I see it as an initiation, a re-arranging, a gaining of new values and casting-off of old ones; when much which was powerful and hidden during life on earth now assumes its true clarity and importance. Death is often thought of as bringing rest and happiness, but these are only two factors in a very complex process, more truly to be regarded as an intensification of living. So I look forward to it and do not fear it at all, though I certainly dislike the prospect of whatever terminal illness might precede it.

Growing old – a process on which I have already embarked – is necessarily much coloured through looking past it to death and beyond. I find old age largely a change of attention, of a highly interesting kind. One is of course constantly losing out in various sorts of 'small change' – people's names formerly so readily recalled now hide themselves, or only pop out at moments chosen by themselves; fingers take it upon themselves to strike the wrong key on the typewriter, or spell a word which begins aright and then changes itself, by some odd association, into another one: there is the spilt wineglass; the general fumbling, the gradual lessening of

13

powers so that one's ambit ever becomes smaller. All these minor misalignments and slowings-down impose themselves against one's will; in one sense they so inexorably and slyly push one down the slope and into the tomb, yet in another hint so clearly of an immediate need and challenge to *refocus* one's attention. It is a fortunate thing that the inevitable onset includes not only this continual falling further and further behind, but also this positive thing. This shift in attention can reveal something so much more interesting in oneself (and of course in others) than was formerly supposed possible. It is that old age makes visible a larger self which stands side by side with the familiar everyday one, and gradually becomes more and more important. The limitations and losses end in showing up this new self more clearly, and, unlike the familiar daily self, this newly-seen self is no inevitable casualty but is indeed the emerging self which will accompany one past the grave, and play the dominant part in one's new life.

During later years one can more and more transfer the centre of attention, the centre of interest, from the self for so long geared closely to earth to this other much more flexible and widely ranging inner self, which has the power to look before and after, and with which that familiar self can steadily bring itself more and more into alignment.

This is something much more than a change of focus brought about by waning interest in life. It is much more important, a tapping of parts of the self one never fully knew existed: a waxing interest, and a growth of the total self.

This change of focus does not of course come about of itself without effort. It is helped by a study and acceptance of certain ideas which have become available in comparatively recent years: not through scientific, medical or formal psychological discoveries, but derived from unusual and unorthodox sources, at present not generally held in high repute. I refer to the much extended panorama painted by communications from discarnate persons; some are closely linked by ties of love to those to whom they are speaking on earth, others are impersonal teachers. This has revolutionised my feelings towards the inevitable declining years and death itself.

The group of ideas falls into two parts: first, comment upon the outer events of one's life on earth, and the drawing attention to factors in them, powerful but hitherto largely hidden; second, the transformations the self will undergo after death, not automatically as the inevitable result of death, but as the result of one's own efforts, travail, and persistent hard work. The work is the measure of the subsequent gain. After death as before it, one only gets what one pays and works for. What faces one is a complete *metanoia*, the finding and growing of a new man in oneself of much extended power, who has to be acquired bit by bit in order to have the skill to face a similarly much extended environment which he will gradually meet with. The Ancient Egyptians pointed to the essence of these concepts in the title of the volume usually translated as *The Book of the Dead* but which is, more correctly, *The Book of Coming Forth into Life*.

Every enquirer needs to ask, of course, whether all this is no more than a lot of nonsense. This can only be answered by saying that the proof of the pudding is in what one is eating, even though one can only eat a small part of this particular pudding now, and the remainder after death. But what does eating the pudding consist of, what is the technique or techniques needed? It is necessary, though by no means easy, for ageing people to get their attention free, and available for facing forward. It is comparatively easy to let go of old tasks, formerly tackled readily, or at least with steady duty, easy to let others take on the burden of the responsibility, but far less easy to grasp the opportunity for an intensification and even a *speeding-up* of one's own consciousness. When young, one heard one's parents say that in spite of their age they did not *feel* any the less young *inside* themselves: a remark greeted by me, and no doubt by other young people, with cheerful contempt. But it is of course true, and is one of those invisible pointers to one's survival of death:

that essentially one is not old, though one's body is, and that one is ready for mental and emotional expansion. It is a valuable discovery to come to believe in one's spiritual youth.

Obviously it is no use directing one's attention forward beyond death merely in anticipation of re-meeting familiar old friends and loved family members. This is often really looking backward not forward, since, just as one changes in the direction of this more real larger self, so do they. This is part of the adventure. It is neither any adventure to us nor any help to them if in thinking of them we mentally imprison them in the old personalities they were, and which since death they have been learning to discard. Not that when we re-meet them we shall no longer know them, as many fear, or that they will, by earlier death, have gone too far away for us to catch up with them. This is untrue, and a fault in earth perspective; for the pathway ahead is a very long one, and at most they will only have taken a few steps along it. We shall recognise them as easily as, late in life, we can recognise a friend of our youth for long unseen. It is their inner self which will have changed and grown, provided they have grasped their opportunities. In a very practical way too, plenty of evidence offers itself of their continued interest in our problems. One measure of *their* advance is whether this demonstrated interest of theirs is focussed upon the growing inward self of ours, or only upon the everyday person. The one still on earth also needs to loosen hold on his old self. If he does not open himself to larger issues, then he limits what can be brought to him by his old friends who have grown. The point is to forge a new relationship, growing out of the old, but with larger horizons. Better still are relationships with guides and teachers, whose existence may have been hitherto unsuspected.

Anyone who faces this expansion of being is likely to encounter the corresponding occult literature, whether at high level or low. He will come across concepts of reincarnation, of the higher self or oversoul, of group souls and group consciousness. An important factor in this literature, some of it profound, some fanciful, some of course merely trivial, is that it is particularly harmonious to this emerging larger self of old age, speaking as it does of the essential agelessness of the soul, whether it be long or short in experience at its present moment of time. The importance of reincarnation is that it looks forward as much as backward. Its meaning has often been grossly distorted. The purpose is not in the least to claim identity with Cleopatra or Napoleon. Glamour must fly out of the window before reincarnation can show its meanings, which are many. These include a diagnosis, as dire as many medical ones, of faults which have grown up in one, the seeds of which have lain in former lives, of refusals, failures and self-regardings, and which it is now urgent to correct before they proliferate further. Many unweeded corners of the garden can present themselves for attention near the end of a life. They can form an unpleasant surprise, for the spiritual lessons of maturity, once faced, usually become steadily harder. The forward-looking elements in reincarnation point to fruits of these old lives which, well-garnered, persist in the oversoul; and point to the present self on earth as a mere fragment of the whole it will later rejoin. This leads to forming a much more detached view of one's present self – combination as it is of dying animal and a being of long spiritual history. Reincarnation as an idea seriously regarded, helps to restore the proper perspective and shows the dying animal as of small importance. Looking before and after is like a draught of larger life, able to fill many meditative hours in later quiet days. The nourishing qualities of these glimpses lie in making for a gradual enlargement of the soul, and though clearly subject to error, this comes to be felt as a basically truthful enlargement.

It is often through the idea of reincarnation too that more mystical aspects of being are approached, and the more personal self seen as a mere episode, the player who fills the front of the stage, but who is never the star. If a man or woman is really the sum of many merely temporary personalities, the resultant self in the heavens will be glimpsed as a deeper, more experienced and wiser self, before whom one is humbled, whose knowledge too is available for use in the present fragmentary life if one wants it strongly enough, by listening to the voice within. Books such as Helen Greaves's *Testimony of Light* tell of how after death these larger areas of being are entered upon, where the self once again knows itself more truly as part of a group, made up of many others, one's peers whose experience becomes part of one's own. One enters here into mysteries, for each step towards these enlargements is a step towards the Oneness of the All, in which we live and move and have our being.

With so much to look forward to, and such intensified living for which to qualify oneself, both now and hereafter; with the ability and opportunity which age brings to live in this inner self, and to share in the inner selves of others, there is little room to lament the relinquished past, and the physically circumscribed present. As to serious illness, who would not wish to escape that? Yet those who do not escape, often speak after death in praise of the high value of this suffering, so worthwhile and enriching, as seen from the aftermath. Here as elsewhere, one can only bow to experience, but certainly old age, whether in shine or gloom, speaks essentially of added inner riches.

Sir Lennox Berkeley

CBE. Composer. Member of BBC Music Staff, 1942-45. Collard Fellowship in Music, 1946. Composition Professor, Royal Academy of Music, London, 1946-1967. Hon. Music Doc., Oxford, 1970.

I used to wonder, when I was a child, how it was possible that elderly people could be so cheerful in view of their rapidly approaching demise. As many of these were probably only about forty, the phenomenon was less astonishing than I thought, but it has struck me since that many people who really have reached old age display considerable serenity and liveliness of mind, and now that I am myself in this category, I find that there are many compensations for advancing years. The fact that one suffers less from the various forms of insecurity or from the violent emotions that beset one in youth is one of them; another the fact that one's individuality is more firmly established and that one no longer cares, or that one cares much less, what other people think of one. There is also the discovery of things that can be enjoyed that one had not taken advantage of earlier. For example, perhaps because of my absorption in music, I had never learned to use my eyes. I now take great pleasure, not only in pictures, but in the visual world in general. I am more aware of the beauty of much that I see around me, of young people, for instance, and of animals. I have more sympathy with other human beings. This, I feel, is something deeper than the easy-going tolerance that is fashionable today and that springs, as often as not, from a lack of conviction about anything, but I am not claiming it as a virtue. It grows, I think, out of one's experience of life, the realization that we

19

are all prone to weakness, and that other people's failings are merely different from one's own.

I have just said that in old age one is no longer a prey to violent emotion, but I find that I am very easily moved by all manner of things to which I never gave a thought when I was young. Even in music, I find much more that I like and even love than I did, though this is not true of contemporary music in which I find less. Certainly as old age has approached I have found more that I can enjoy in general through knowing more and having a greater experience of life. This sums up the advantages that I have encountered.

The disadvantages are much more obvious. Even if one is still in reasonably good health, one is aware of ebbing vitality and of tiring much more quickly – I can neither work for as many hours nor walk as far – and it is sad that just when one has become more appreciative and more sure in one's estimate of the relative value of things, one no longer has the energy to take advantage of it. Mental and physical fatigue overtakes one, and is not easy to come to terms with. Yeats, in one of his poems, speaks of his soul as 'fastened to a dying animal'. He felt that physical decline was accompanied by increasing mental awareness, and refers often to how much he suffered from opposite states of mind and body. The state of the body, of course, becomes of paramount importance in old age for it can make the whole difference to one's desire to go on living.

It seems that many older people living in retirement suffer from boredom and not knowing what to do with themselves, even if perfectly healthy. This is, to me, inconceivable; I am acutely aware of having only a limited future left and little time in which to do so much: books I want to read, places to see and work to do. I think it was only when I reached seventy, last year, that I began to feel this at all strongly and to regret the amount of time I had wasted in my younger days, and the slow pace at which I had developed, musically and otherwise.

A man's attitude to death is of necessity largely determined by whether or not he has any religious belief. Those who believe, as I do, in the Christian doctrine of life after death are bound to feel differently, both from those who believe rather vaguely in some sort of survival, and from those for whom death means extinction. I have been a Roman Catholic for the greater part of my life, and am thereby committed to the Church's teaching. Though deeply conscious of utter failure to live up to what I believe, the fact of believing it has been an immense happiness, and one that in my better moments banishes the fear of death. This does not mean that I do not dread the anguish of parting from those I love or that I do not have doubts and difficulties, but I am convinced that we should be resigned to the fact that our understanding, in this life, is limited, and that disbelief involves quite as many intellectual difficulties as any religion known to me. There is much to be said for the attitude of the recruit, Feeble, in *King Henry IV*: 'I care not,' he says, 'a man can die but once; we owe God a death'. The feeling that death is part of the natural order of things, that it is a debt that must be paid in return for the gift of life is not unreasonable, for we would surely not prefer never to have existed at all. Even those who cannot reconcile themselves to any religious belief may well be able to agree with the many philosophers of the past, and some, no doubt of the present, who believe that the better part of man can live on after death.

Sir John Betjeman

Kt : 1969, CBE : 1960; C Lit, 1968; Poet and Author. Poet Laureate since 1972. Press Attaché, Dublin, 1941-42; Admiralty, 1943. A Governor of Pusey House, Church of England. Hon. Fellow, Keble College, Oxford, 1972. Hon. LLD (Aberdeen); Hon. D Litt (Oxon, Reading, Birmingham, Liverpool); Hon. ARIBA D Litt, Trinity College (Dublin).

The Commander

On a shining day of October we remembered you,
                                         Commander,
    When the trees were gold and still
And some of their boughs were green where the whip
    of the wind had missed them
    On this nippy Staffordshire hill.

A clean sky streamed through institutional windows
    As we heard the whirr of Time
Touching our Quaker silence, in builders lorries departing
    For Newcastle-under-Lyme.

The proving words of the psalm you bequeathed to the
    gowned assembly
    On waiting silence broke,
Lord, I am not high-minded. . . ' In the youthful voice
                           of the student
    Your own humility spoke.

I remembered our shared delight in architecture and nature
    As bicycling we went
By saffron-spotted palings to crumbling box-pewed
    churches
    Down hazel lanes in Kent.

I remembered on winter evenings, with wine and the
    family round you,
Your reading Dickens aloud
And the laughs we used to have at your gift for
    administration.
    For you were never proud.

Sky and sun and the sea! the greatness of things was in you
    And thus you refrained your soul.
Let others fuss over academical detail,
    You saw people whole.

'Lord, I am not high-minded. . . ' The final lesson you
    taught me,
    When you bade the world good-bye,
Was humbly and calmly to trust in the soul's survival
    When my own hour comes to die.

(John Betjeman's *Collected Poems*, enlarged edition; John
Murray, London)

On the death of a friend

And so the reckoning day has come
For my old friend but not for me
No wonder I am feeling glum
Were he in my place so'ld be he.

Douglas Brown

Assistant Editor, 'Daily Telegraph'.

My favourite verse of Betjeman's was quoted by the *Times* when he was created Poet Laureate. It exquisitely spans the 'generation gap' we speak so much about today:

So looked my father at the last
Right in my soul before he died
Though words we spoke went heedless past
As London traffic-roar outside.
And now the same blue eyes I see
Look through me from a little son
So questioning, so searchingly
That youthfulness and age are one.

Last year, at the age of sixty-four, I suffered a coronary thrombosis, and thought I was going to die. Two little grand-daughters came, as it was supposed, to say goodbye to me in hospital. They were still young enough to be 'trailing clouds of glory', and they looked at me with wonder but with perfect composure. I imagined they were welcoming me home in the name of two of our sons who, a generation ago, died in infancy. Suddenly, life and death seemed all of a piece, like night and morning. I did not feel the need to call to mind any eschatological doctrines taught to me as a Roman Catholic. The prospect of death simply took its place in the total scheme of things, as an harmonious link between time and eternity. Christ's resurrection was no longer a mere dogma; it was an all-embracing reality.

A dress rehearsal for death, such as I experienced, robs the coming actual event of most of its terrors. Fear of the judgment remains, for us sinners, though even that had seemed to be mercifully removed at the time. As for what I may call the nostalgic fears, associated with the slipping away of all familiar things — do not these pertain more to life than to death? Life is full of partings and bereavements; it is a whole succession of 'last times'. Death blots them out, and subsumes them into 'the white radiance of eternity'.

Towards the end of a normal life the road winds steeply down hill. Pain and disability are probable, as well as the deeper kinds of human loneliness. We cannot easily bear these otherwise hopeless burdens, I think, if in our thoughts we deliberately isolate them from their inevitable consummation.

Some ageing people push death out of their minds altogether, pretending it does not exist. Others wrap it in a morbid romanticism, falsely separating it from the life with which it is intimately bound up. The best way is to accept it as little children do. Their birth is like our demise, and we return the way they came. What a privilege we have enjoyed meanwhile, however much we may have abused it!

The Reverend Anthony Bullen

Since 1964 Director of Religious Education for the Archdiocese of Liverpool. Writer, lecturer.

He was nearing sixty. That very day his secretary had said to him, 'I wouldn't like to live to be fifty'. She expressed the sentiment with the hushed awe of a person who is aghast at a possible but awful fate. Unconsciously she had paid him a compliment because, sensitive girl though she was, she must not have adverted to his age. Did this mean that he didn't appear to be as old as he really was?

He was listening to a concert on his radio: Brahms' Fourth Symphony. How old was Brahms when he wrote this symphony, he wondered. Over fifty for sure! The ripe fruit of a life-time of music-making. He went over to the bookcase and took down *Music of the World*. But the book gave no indication of the composer's age at the time this symphony was written.

All right, then. So I'm on the downward path, he thought. Stiffness in the joints, slowness of reactions, slight deafness. 'Poor old chap', his nephews and nieces would say, 'He's past it, you know. Active in his time but now . . . '

But there was a credit side to approaching old age. He had already experienced the unexpected bonus of this time of life, the liberation from wondering (or caring about, for that matter) what sort of impression he was making on people. Of course, such unconcern had its dangers. It could imply an imperviousness to criticism, an irresponsible complacency. But once one was aware of this danger, the likelihood of self-delusion was lessened.

He had always understood that unconcern about the opinion of others was a sign of maturity. Strange to think of maturity at his time of life. Surely one should be mature much earlier in life than at nearly sixty. On the other hand, one speaks about a really old wine as 'mature'.

I suppose I still am growing in maturity, he mused, even at my age. After all that's the purpose and end of it all. He picked up a copy of the New Testament and began to search through the letter to the Ephesians. Yes, this was the passage. 'In this way,' wrote Paul, 'we are all to come to unity in our faith and in our knowledge of the Son of God until we become the perfect Man, fully mature with the fulness of Christ himself.'

'Fully mature with the fulness of Christ himself'. Well, that won't be reached this side of the grave. Of that he was sure. But at least he had consciously been aiming at it over the years. He had daily tried to leave himself to the transforming power of the Spirit, having long since recognised that Heaven was written on its gates – 'No immature people allowed here'. So he tried over the years to slough off the petty immaturities, stupid competitiveness, over-sensitivity to criticism, a tendency to bore people with his news and views – all these traits were, in his estimation, indications of immaturity. But there was no doubt he still had a long way to go.

He hadn't really begun seriously to think about the wrench of physical death. Not that he was afraid of it. He was even prepared to accept the indignity of it all. He often recalled his mother's death – three weeks of disintegration. 'She would be kept alive for another month', the doctor had said, 'if you put her in a nursing home. But wouldn't you rather have her die at home with her family around her?' Well, his death would not be like that. Hardly possible for there to be any family around him. A nurse, a sister, perhaps.

He'd always hero-worshipped the Apostle, Paul. And he pictured him now, in the dark dank Mammertine prison in Rome, writing pathetically to his friends. 'Do your best to come and see me as soon as you can . . . only Luke is with me. When you come, bring the cloak I left with Carpus in Troas . . . and the scrolls, especially the parchment ones'. But Paul knew in his heart that the end was at hand. 'As for me, my life is already being poured away as a libation and the time has come for me to be gone. I have fought the good fight to the end; I have run the race to the finish; I have kept the faith; all there is to come now is the crown of righteousness reserved for me, which the Lord, the righteous judge will give to me on that Day; and not only to me but to all those who have longed for his Appearing'. (2 Timothy)

Too early yet for him to be able to speak so confidently. But it was something for him to aim at.

The symphony ended and the audience applauded enthusiastically. Then there was silence in the room except for the ticking of a clock and the distant hum of traffic. But the silence was more than an absence of sound. He was aware of a presence . . .

The Rt Reverend B.C. Butler

OSB. Auxiliary Bishop of Westminster since 1966. Headmaster of Downside School, 1940-46. Abbot of Downside, 1946-66. Writer, theologian.

Timor mortis conturbat me, sings the poet; the fear of death dismayeth me. And the Author to the Hebrews speaks of those who through fear of death were subject to bondage throughout their lives.

As a boy and a young man I found little echo of such fear within me. That all men die, and that I was a man, were propositions to which I gave a notional assent; but as far as feelings and fears or expectations went, it was as though I were everlasting. There is a kind of conspiracy in our modern western culture to hide the grim fact of death away, as though it were something indecent. Perhaps the prudishness is itself a hidden compliment to the fearfulness of death and the obscenity of dying.

One can, for a time, but with less success as one grows older, avert one's face from the certainty of one's own death. But the deaths of others will keep breaking in upon our unnatural serenity. In a long corridor of the abbey of St Paul's outside the Walls, Rome, they have fixed to the wall fragments of Roman inscriptions, discovered for the most part in the vicinity of the abbey. One of these, I think a pagan one, runs somewhat as follows: 'Valeria, aged thirteen years two months seven days; her parents, mourning'. Somehow, the simplicity, the brevity, the unconnectedness of this cry of uncomprehending anguish from the past, has moved me to actual tears. How can pure love exist along with the meaningless absurdity of extinction?

29

The civilised pagans of an earlier age than ours did look death in the face, and they found that its visage was monstrous. Lucretius tried the short way out. He argued that the fear of death was a quite illusory fear, not because death is not a fact, but because the fear supposes in some contradictory way that we shall survive to lament our own extinction. He offers some thirty 'proofs' that there is no immortality, and concludes as though on a note of triumph: *Nil igitur mors est ad nos neque pertinet hilum*; death, then, is nothing so far as we are concerned, and has no relation to us at all. He imagines a lament over a man who has just died: 'Never again will your home welcome you with joy; never again will your wife and your darling children hasten to win your first kiss and pierce your heart with silent joy. Never will you enjoy prosperity nor give protection to those you love. Unhappy man, one disastrous day has taken from you everything that makes life worth while'. And his reply is: 'Yes, but then you will no longer have any desire for these things'. In saying which, I venture to think that Lucretius missed a point. It is here, today, while love is still vigorous and sweet, that the menace of extinction aims its blow at the significance of love itself. Love claims everlastingness, not just because it is something good which we should like to prolong, but because if death is the end of everything love cannot be itself even today. It is all very well to tell a man to build his hopes on a foundation of absolute and unshakeable despair; but love cannot be built upon such a foundation. If death is the end, then human life is absurd. But absurdity is something that can neither be lived nor escaped from – since suicide is itself an absurd affirmation of some inverted value.

Thus it is that the Christian good news ('Christ has been raised from the dead, the first fruits of all humanity') not only rang out like a message of hope to a beleaguered city in the world to which it was first addressed, but still today challenges our attention as not just an anodyne for evanescent sorrows and childish fears but a possible resolution of a contradiction that lies at the heart of our experience. If we were incapable of reflection, death would not worry but only, in moments of peril, frighten us. It is as thinking creatures that we are fascinated and appalled and threatened by the fact of death. And it is as thinking creatures that we can, grace helping us, attain to the Easter faith. For Christ himself has died; but he has risen and 'death has no more dominion over him'.

Lord David Cecil

CH. Companion of Literature. Goldsmith's Professor of English Literature, Oxford, 1948–1970. Rede Lecturer, Cambridge University, 1955. Don, biographer, critic. Hawthornden Prize. James Tait Black Memorial Prize.

I am seventy-two years old; and I ask myself how do I now feel about old age and death? My first thought is that the two things are different: my reaction to each must be discussed separately. Let me begin with age. Here Gibbon speaks better for me than I can speak for myself. At the close of his autobiography, he says: 'I will not suppose any premature decay of the mind or the body; but I must reluctantly observe that two causes, the abbreviation of time and the failure of hope, will always tinge with a browner shade the evening of life'. How right he is! Myself, I am lucky enough not yet to have experienced any marked decay of mind or body; yet my attitude to old age is different from what it would have been ten years ago.

Various things account for this. First of all the fate of my contemporaries, especially my older contemporaries. Many of them have aged visibly and some of them have died. Observing them, I have grown accustomed to see the process of life reach its final stage in those who I have known since they were young and strong. Secondly, the world around me has changed greatly from what it was in my youth; so that I now realise that I belong to the past. The moral and social assumptions generally taken for granted when I was young have largely vanished with the consequence that the opinions I built on them have had their foundations undermined. As a result, I feel mentally more solitary. Because I have fewer relations and close friends living, there are fewer people to whom I can speak with a certainty of being understood. Because I am no longer, as it were, a native of the age I live in, I no longer hold opinions with the particular confidence that comes from knowing that they are generally accepted opinions.

Finally my attitude has been changed by what Gibbon calls 'the abbreviation of time and the failure of hope'. It is no longer possible to look forward and this means that I am deprived of the pleasures that come from looking forward; the pleasure of planning for the future, the pleasure of making a new friend with the prospect of a longer friendship. The old have to learn to live in the present. Sidney Smith once advised a friend: 'Take short views of life – as far as dinner or tea'. I have often thought this true. I think it truer, now that I am seventy-two.

That I should do so is a gain. Indeed there are compensations in growing old. It enables one to be more detached for one thing – especially about public affairs. I used to be very much worried by reading bad news in the papers about the political future. Now I realise that any future, political or otherwise, is not going to be a long future for me. It is therefore silly for me to worry about it. Moreover I find it easier to see public events in a longer perspective and as brief incidents in the mysterious, unending course of human history; a course which goes through good and bad phases but in which nothing gets better or worse for ever. To recognise this creates a soothing feeling of detachment.

Detachment also makes one realise that one's own personal success or failure is, in the long view, of little importance, so that it is foolish to worry about them. As a very large part of the worries of life are concerned with one's own success or failure, this is a great gain. Another gain is a growth in the pleasures of memory. If I have little to look forward to, I have much to look back on and almost all of it I find interesting – also new. Proust was right in thinking, that experience is often at its most precious when recollected; for then it is illuminated by the knowledge of what came after.

Moreover, memory tells one such absorbing and informative stories. It is extraordinarily interesting to trace the lives of people one has known since youth and to note the virtues and weaknesses, the pressures and chances which have determined the course of their lives. Only those who have sat through a human drama to the end of its last act can discover its full significance.

Nor are the pleasures of memory the only pleasures of old age. For me delight in the beauties of art and nature is as strong as ever it was. Perhaps they produce fewer moments of intense ecstasy than in youth, but their effect is steady and consoling; all the more because it has survived when other pleasures have faded. If I can no longer enjoy a game of tennis or a late evening party as I once did, I continue to delight in a fine day or in listening to music. The fact that I do so has for me a result of the first importance: it helps to confirm me in an ultimate faith in the things of the spirit. Life in this world alike for the race and the individual, has shown up as transient and unsatisfying; an unfading response to the beautiful, therefore, seems evidence of the existence of a spiritual reality beyond this world and immune from the chances and changes of this mortal life.

So much for age, what about death? Here I feel differently from what I did as a young man. Then I was terrified by the idea of death. The thought that every second that passed was a second less of life struck a chill to my heart. Now the chill has evaporated, to be succeeded by a sense of tranquil acceptance. I feel with Bacon that 'it is as natural to die as to be born'. The death of friends and relations, saddening in other ways, is calming in this context. I see that they have not been cut off untimely, that their life has run its full and natural course. So also my own life will have soon run its course: it cannot be long before my own time will have come. This thought is restful. Nothing, however, is to be had for nothing in this hard world. Knowing more about death means knowing more about the process of dying. This is a disturbing knowledge. It is the old man not the youth who prays for an easy death.

These thoughts about old age and death are, I know, commonplace. But at seventy-two years old they come fresh to one.

Mrs Sebastian Comper

Née Countess Zoë Ozurk. Russian emigrée.

Years go by,
expecting life to burst
upon a young beginning.
Devoid of aim,
Heart waking, mind apart
waiting for what chance,
or fate, may bring.

Years go by,
life gives abundantly
and takes away . . .
teaching to forget the hurt
and bless the gift –
Experience gratefully obtained;
with aim ahead – no further drift.

Years gone by,
the end in sight
comes gently as a lamb
the Master's voice obeying
towards the Light.
All falls in line
with inner happiness attained.

Dominic Cooper (aged 30)

Trevelyan Scholarship, Oxford. Author.

I have always been fascinated by the very young and the very old.

I have no desire to denigrate the spectacular glories of a man – or woman – in what is called the prime of his life, for the sheer dynamism of him striking out into his uncharted future cannot fail to convey itself to others. But this central, most highly active, section of his life is so often confused, so often masked by the unconscious attitudinising, by the trying on of new styles and faces as he attempts to find himself that the true personality is not always clearly defined. The fire and clamour are exciting and impressive but also concealing. Nor do I discount the stages of adolescence and middle age for they are often decisive turning points: but they are basically transitional and therefore deceptive. The former is painfully tedious, full of disproportion both in hope and fear, as one looks forward impatiently towards an adulthood that refuses to come; while the latter with its first desperate glances back over the shoulder through the distorted focus of nostalgia and the growing need to accept both a waning physique and the younger world's quiet rejection of oneself – this, too, catches a person in a phase of change and unrest.

But in the very young and the very old we are presented with people in states of relative simplicity, in states which bear a strange similarity. We say that as a person grows old he or she reverts to his roots . . . and is it by chance that we euphemistically refer to dotage as a 'second childhood'?

In a child we see a true, if still germinal, form for a child knows nothing of either affectation or dissembling: it says what it feels, cries when it wants to cry, laughs when it wants to laugh, all with neither thought nor care for the consequences. Only in growing up does it acquire the sadly necessary defence mechanism of circumspection. Old age can never refind the same pureness of being for the mind, like the bones, has been shaped and made brittle by the years; but as the active part of life recedes it often carries away with it much of the outer layers, the gangue, the matrix and once again the little speck of ore is revealed – hardened, chipped, crystallised perhaps but still the essence of the creature. There is this simple, elemental structure in the process of living which intimates that our destination is no more than a reflection of our point of departure. In both cases the state of non-existence lies close at hand and the creature is distanced from the world, withdrawn into the silence of its inner being. If I am predominantly concerned with these opening and closing chapters of life it is because they contain the clearest outlines of whatever is true in us, both in the individual himself and in the broader concept of each of us in relation to the *primum mobile*.

The state of childhood is only interesting in retrospect. The young child's life is one of pure sensation which precludes any awareness of a possibility that not long ago he did not exist. When I passed the age of still hankering for the happy innocence of childhood (the innocence is genuine; the happiness, or enjoyment of the innocence, is a nostalgic illusion) I quickly turned about and looked inquisitively into the distant future. But I was, and still am, incapable of envisaging the details of my old age and death and so I had to content myself with forming an idea of them in more objective terms. I observed, listened, thought and gleaned information from whatever was available.

To my age, being old is not an immediate problem. Death may come any time but the problem of being old is only too easily shelved. I cannot believe that anyone looks forward to the inevitable aches and pains of growing old, even less to the possible physical agonies of what is so coldly termed a terminal disease. And indeed there is little that can be said that could turn such things into a pleasant prospect. They must simply be faced with sheer courage, a courage that is to be learned and practised from the day one is born. A fear of the actual process of dying is minimally assuaged by the thought that by the time it comes upon us we shall probably be tired and not so desperate to cling to life. Cold comfort, perhaps, and not true in all cases.

Apart from the actual physical suffering of old age, each person also has to reconcile himself to the emotional idea of growing old and dying – of the mechanism gradually running down and finally, with an incontrovertible, dull click, stopping. A person's attitude towards life depends on his attitude towards old age and death; and his attitude towards old age and death depends on his beliefs as to what happens after death. I am a Christian with an unshakeable belief in an afterlife. No complex theories of reincarnation or metempsychosis or whatever: just an old-fashioned faith in the soul's return to its Creator. An antiquated idea for these days, perhaps, but neither mockery nor scientific 'proof' to the contrary can disturb my faith, a faith which can be neither credit nor discredit to me but just a fact which I happen to see as a blessing.

And with this belief, the prospect of death – and its prologue, old age – suddenly becomes not just acceptable but exciting. Compared to the few decades we have in this life, an afterlife unbounded by our concepts of time becomes of major importance to anyone who happens to believe in it. I must, however, stress that I in no way despise life. To the contrary, I am a romantic, a sensual person willing and, I believe, able to enjoy and hold precious everything that this world has to offer. I can laugh and suffer and love without limits, I can stand outside myself with elation. But I always carry the thought that it will all pass, probably many years away in the future but possibly before I can finish the next word. I think of the persons I love, of the things I plan and long to do and I literally cannot accept that death may deprive me of them . . . and yet, at the same time, the old thought goes through my head: 'Have I only minutes to go?'

Death, seen in a negative fashion, as a destroyer of life, is unbearable. So unbearable that many people shun the thought or mention of it, only to shake and howl inwardly as it finally creeps up on them. But liberty lies in acceptance not in flight and if you can see your way to accepting it positively, regarding it as a gateway into a state of peace and contentment that will transcend anything experienced in this life then, suddenly and apocalyptically, it is no longer a demon lurking in every shadow but a laughing, embracing friend. I love life and I love death: in this there is no contradiction but the essence of the endless dichotomy of human existence. There is no need to reconcile these apparent opposites. Only when I grasp them both simultaneously do I feel myself to be a complete human being.

With this view of death, which I have not acquired through laborious ratiocination but which simply crept up beside me like a friendly companion, the prospect of growing old takes on a new and almost mystical appearance. This will never cure the pains of old-age, loneliness and disability but it can be an effective spiritual salve for the coming wounds. I, like everyone else, shall groan and curse at the day-to-day suffering. I shall feel the exhaustion and irritation as I totter out to the shops. I shall suffer from the damp and cold. I shall worry over lack of money. I shall watch friends and family die and feel myself isolated in a world that needs me less and less every day. These will be different pains from those I have experienced so far but they will be dominated by the criterion which I now hold for my life. Namely, that one's duty lies in the obligation to keep going, to keep going as best one can. If one can get by, somehow, with the nearest thing to a smile on one's face, if one can doggedly stick to one's ideals and never totally despair then one has achieved all that can be expected. To have done this through one's life will enhance the mystical aspect of growing old. There will be the sensation of having passed through the fire, of having been tempered and burnished in preparation for a new and more complete existence and from this, I believe, there will come a new peace. People talk endlessly of happiness and mean many different things – excitement, elation, joy – but for me happiness is peace. Of having come to terms with myself and the rest of the world, however grim either may sometimes seem. And peace should be the ruling factor of old age. But it is not something which can be cultivated in one's last years and it is vital that it should be sought out and developed early in life so that when the new struggles of the pre-death era arrive, one is prepared and strong. We must live our lives in love and joy and with the image of the end that is the beginning always before us.

Martin Cooper

CBE. Music critic, writer, broadcaster.

Old age is a set of physical facts, a condition of the human organism that may be postponed, ameliorated, even to some extent ignored, but cannot by any means be finally avoided. The experience of ageing is something that it is fortunately impossible to imagine; and what has been written about old age, though perfectly intelligible to the middle-aged and even to the young, fails to carry any conviction because it always seems to describe another race of beings, some different order of creation. No young man really believes that he will one day be the double of the codger now blocking his path at the office or on the motorway. And if women are both more realistic and more physically aware than men, it is still impossible for a woman of thirty really to grasp, even in imagination, the fact that she will one day be the woman of seventy, stripped of her physical attractions as an autumn tree is stripped of its leaves and, like the tree, exposing the shapeliness or unshapeliness of her personality without ornament or disguise.

'*Nec lamentari nec indignari, sed intelligere*' (No lamenting or indignation – try to understand) – Leonardo's motto is the right prescription for the malady of growing old. Whatever seems disturbing or saddening, either in the decay of personal faculties or in the state of society, should be studied objectively, without lamenting over past glories or indignation over present depravities, neither quite so glorious nor quite so depraved as they seem to the old. The first step towards acceptance is understanding, and to refuse to accept the inevitable is to remain profoundly immature.

Death is different, because death is not only a physical, but a metaphysical fact. No one, however old, can know for certain how he will face dying – the call to abandon absolutely everything that is known and familiar, the unconditional surrender of even that dearest, closest and only truly inseparable companion, one's own body. If physical death is indeed the end of the individual, human dignity demands at least a stoical surrender, a dénouement not beneath the level of the rest of the drama. The hope of another life, outside the conditions of time and space and therefore inconceivable by the human imagination but not for that reason impossible, is an integral part of many great religions, palliating the pain of growing old and removing all but the purely physical, animal fear of dying. If the religious man's interpretation of human existence is the true one, that truth will already have largely transformed his life before he comes to die: and whether or not after the death of the body he receives the confirmation of his faith in another existence, he can hope to have experienced at least something of that 'infinite superabundance of the divine mercy, already secretly present here below in its entirety' (Simone Weil). Not only virtue, but faith too is its own reward.

Georgina Denison (aged 25)

Publisher's publicity manager.

I find the prospect of old age very depressing, in spite of the encouraging examples of it that I have been lucky enough to know. In every case, though, it seems to me that the old are lessened, rather than increased, by their age. So, emotionally, it is a saddening spectacle, and on a larger, more impersonal scale, old age is a tragedy. The present problem seems to be the position of the old person on the fringes of society; supported by it and yet excluded, like a child. That comparison is the bitterest irony of all, for while the child is cherished partly because of the possibilities latent in him, the old person's qualities are on the wane.

There have, of course, been societies which greatly honoured their elders, but basically, I think, for the practical reasons that the old were the possessors of the knowledge or of the wealth of the community. The situation seems unlikely to recur in our rapidly moving society, which is also one in which it becomes increasingly difficult, and, I hope decreasingly necessary, to amass a fortune. We have also invented machines for storing information which surpass the human brain in capacity and efficiency.

It seems that the best solution for the old is to continue to play an active role in the community for as long as possible. Here I am halted in my ruminations about 'old' as a synonym for 'useless' by the thought of Churchill, aged seventy in 1944, and then by a procession of magnificent old men: Russell, Rubinstein, Picasso, Casals. They were exceptional people, but I can't help feeling that their continued vitality was partly due to their being able to continue in their chosen occupation.

It seems that women adapt better than men to old age. Presumably this is because the men are more used to playing an active role in the world, while women are, on the whole, conditioned to living in a smaller sphere - and personal power matters less to them.

The first proof of our humanity lies in our treatment of those who are of no apparent 'use' to us, and our behaviour towards our old people casts a rather gloomy light on our civilisation. The pensions are appalling, but loneliness seems to be the chief complaint – and every one of us could help to remedy this. Although it is easier to talk to others of one's age, or race, the extra effort involved in more difficult communications often leads to interesting reassessments of one's own ideas.

Another unpleasant side to old age must, I suspect, be a knowledge of failure, which must come to everyone. Every small success achieved is also a disappointment: a disappointment that the feat was possible, which negates the effort put towards it. How much more bitter it must be to survey one's whole life and judge it! But perhaps as in childhood one is too aware of life's complexity to judge it. Only extreme youth has the arrogance to talk in terms of black and white, success and failure. The loss of friends and equals must also be a hard one; the lack of those who can justifiably criticise could make one feel like a rather irrelevant idol – a household god. I imagine that the proverbial wisdom of age is accompanied by a sense of futility. Apart from a natural and almost inevitable cynicism, it must be hard to find a purpose to which it would seem worthwhile to devote one's last remaining years.

All in all, it seems a gloomy prospect, but perhaps there is truth in Freud's theory of man's longing to return to an inorganic state. Then increasing immobility, the cessation of demands made on one, and the sense that no further achievements are necessary, could bring their own rewards.

Finally, I remember my grandmother, whose old age I was about to wish on everybody; until I recall that it would seem a hard one. Her son was killed in World War II, her daughters were scattered over England; in her last years she moved from house to flat to hotel room. She died painfully of cancer. But I think she was the gayest, kindest, most generous person I have ever met. Her children and grandchildren adored her, and it came as a shock when one remembered, occasionally, her age. She swam in the English sea every day from March until October, she played bridge better and did the *Times* crossword puzzle faster than any other member of the family. She played boisterous games of Racing Demon on the floor until her grandchildren, at a very late age, grew out of it. She took me out from school on Sundays and helped me to smuggle sweets past fearsome matrons, and she took me to see the X-certificate films which were such a necessary status symbol to a fourteen year old. We discussed sex, politics, books, money, life – any subject – with only an occasional reminder of the changes which had taken place between her youth and mine. If I could discover the secret of her old age, then I would feel qualified to write about it.

William Douglas Home

Playwright, author.

Old age and death you bid me write about
Which means arthritis, blood-pressure and gout
And funerals and tears and worms and shrouds
But I would rather write about great clouds
Billowing ever heavenwards on which
The good, the bad, the beauty and the witch,
The criminal, the saint, all, day and night
Twang their eternal harps in wild delight.

Dame Daphne du Maurier

DBE. Author.

'To grow old is more difficult than to die, because to ren-
ounce a good once and for all, costs less than to renew the
sacrifice day by day and in detail. To bear with one's own
decay, to accept one's lessening capacity, is a harder and rarer
virtue than to face death. To know how to grow old is the
master-work of wisdom, and one of the most difficult chapters in the great art of living'.

This quotation from Amiel's *Journal* comes from a little
book printed in 1906, entitled *Character and Conduct*. There
is a Thought for each day of the year, and the quote above
is dated December 27, the same day on which I write these
lines, in 1973. It has not been an easy Christmas for old
people. They have been told in their newspapers, over the
radio, and on their television sets if they possess one, that
fuel is scarce, that lights burn low, that food is dear, and
remembering war-time they are the first to refrain from putting on the fire the extra lump of coal that might bring
warmth; the first to switch off the electric light bulb that
brings cheer to the living-room or bedroom, the first to put
aside the saucepan of milk and leave it unheated on the stove.

Across the road the lights shine brightly from the windows
of the younger folk who do not remember 1940 – who were
perhaps not even born. Cars roll by despite shortage of pe-
trol. 'The government got us into this mess. Let them get us
out of it'. Let's eat, drink, and be merry, for tomorrow we

die. Only the young won't die, not yet. The old will. This year . . . next year?

Here within a radius of four miles there are four old people that I love dearly and know well. One is my aunt and god-mother, aged ninety-six. The second my father's cousin, she is ninety-four. The third my faithful friend and gardener of ninety-one. The fourth a youngster in comparison, only eighty-two, but blind and unsteady on her legs. The first three live in their own homes, the last in a Home for Old People.

All four are totally unlike in character. My aunt, my mother's sister, never married. She was one of those devoted daughters who selflessly looked after her parents until death, and at the same time worked as secretary to my actor father. Her family were all in all to her. I can never remember her harassed or ill-tempered. She loved all animals, her succession of little dogs bore witness to the fact. She was, is, highly religious. Her Anglican faith has never wavered. Once, when teasing her about her age, she answered, smiling 'I really don't know why I have lived so long, I'm sure I don't deserve it'.

But she does. Happiness enfolds her like the shawl around her shoulders, and if these last months and weeks she has sometimes been confused it is not a turbulent confusion, more a probing back into the past, murmuring to herself the names of brothers, sisters, cousins, long since dead. 'Am I the only one left?' she asks, puzzled. 'Of your generation, yes', I tell her. 'Oh, well . . there it is', she answers, 'never mind, you are here, and you (to her devoted nurse) and you', to the smiling housekeeper, 'and you', to the small dog on her lap, 'the last of all the others that went before.

Is it her natural character that has kept her happy? Or her faith in God and the hereafter? I do not know.

My cousin has been a widow for many years. She had one daughter, an actress, and the daughter died of cancer in her mid-forties. My cousin liked nothing so much as travel. Austria, Italy . . . a bohemian to her finger-tips she was never so happy as when dossing down in a strange hotel, meeting new people (but they had to be intelligent 'I can't abide fools, never could' she mutters) and now, far from the actors, writers, artists that she knew and could pit her wits against, she sits all day in her chair in her ground-floor flat wondering what foolish whim induced her to end her days in Cornwall. 'If I were in London,' she tells me, 'I could at least go to the opera'. But she couldn't. And she knows it.

My cousin is incontinent, and there can surely be no greater disability and shame for someone who all her life has been sharp-witted and intolerant, than to be swathed day and night in padded napkins like an infant.

She was born and brought up a Roman Catholic, educated in a convent which she hated. Today she has no faith. Is this partly the cause of her restless state of mind, or does the root cause lie with her basic personality? I do not know. Sometimes we have discussed death which she fears.

'Don't worry,' I tell her, 'either you, all of us, will be snuffed out like candles and there will be no more pain, like sleep; or you will find yourself arriving at some Other World airport or station, and your Papa and Mama will be there, and your husband, and your daughter, all your friends to greet you, and it will be more marvellous than anything you ever knew in life'.

'H'm', she ponders, 'I hope Sybil won't be there. I never cared for Sybil'. (Sybil was her eldest sister. They never got on.) 'Sybil,' I suggest, 'will have the tact to stay away'.

Later though, I can't help feeling, if my vision is correct, Sybil will aid her sibling through unchartered seas, and my cousin will know gratitude at last.

Skip (short for Skipper) has known many trades. He has looked after horses, cattle, pigs; he has been to sea, he has tended woodlands, raised vegetables, and now in the evening of his days at ninety-one catches a 'bus twice a week and comes to chop wood in my cellar and fill log baskets. In summer he hoes the drive. A life-long Methodist he attends chapel every Sunday, and shakes his head at the dwindling attendance. 'T'iddent what it used to be', he tells me, 'I don't know what's wrong with the world these days. Nobody want to work neither'. If Skip stayed home in his snug little house and didn't come to chop wood he would soon fade, and dwindle away, like the chapel congregation. I have this on good authority from his loving wife, and I can see it for myself.

'See you Monday', I tell him before the weekend, and he nods and smiles, 'See you Monday, lady', and he returns home a little more breathless perhaps, a little more bent about the shoulders, but satisfied, content. He can still do a man's job in a man's way. This is his reason for living.

Shirley was the daughter of a schoolmaster. She herself taught music when she was young. In middle-age she and the friend with whom she lived were bombed out of London, and came down to live in a cottage in Menabilly woods. The friend, the more dominant character, was inclined to banish Shirley to the back when visitors came, so that she herself could hog the conversation. When the friend died Shirley continued to live on her own in the cottage in the woods. A high Anglican, like my aunt, the visit of the parish priest was the great event of her solitary life. And listening to music on the radio. Then her eyes, always her weakest feature, began to fail. Her legs too became swollen. She stumbled her way about downstairs, feeling the walls, but it was no longer safe for her home-help to leave her long alone.

'I don't want to be a nuisance to anyone', she said, and it was her own decision, taken with great courage, to go into the Home near St Austell.

She has been there now for a number of years, and though it was hard at first to become one of a community with whom she has not a great deal in common, she has a room to herself, and is reconciled. She has means enough to hire a car twice a week to take her to church. This is her great consolation.

When I visit her we have tremendous discussions on the Apostolic Succession, about which I am ill-informed and she is passionate, and I am pretty sure that if we talked of an after-life, and I suggested my theory of a celestial airport, she might be deeply shocked. Nothing but St Peter at the golden gates, with a choir of angels in the background, would content her.

A childhood companion of mine, well-loved, who was discovered in middle life to be schizophrenic, wrote to me once from his self-imposed enclosure that he believed when we die we all attain the heaven we desire. My aunt will find her family and a pack of little dogs, their tails wagging in welcome. Skip his horses and his cattle, and a full congregation, John Wesley with outstretched hand. Shirley the heavenly host and a singing choir. My cousin? An Austrian castle I hope, peopled with princelings, poets, and dramatists.

The writer May Sinclair had a less happy theory. She wrote a short story which I read when I was young suggesting that in the after-life we continue the action that most excited us over and over again throughout eternity. In the story her heroine, who had once committed adultery with her lover in a strange hotel, found herself, in death, in that same hotel corridor approaching a bedroom door. She could not escape, whichever way she turned. The act must be repeated, not once, not twice, but forever and forever. Neither boredom, nor hatred, nor disgust, could bring cessation. I find this frightening. Not a tale for the aged. As eventide approaches most of us cling to familiar things. The routine to which we have become accustomed. Meals on the stroke of the hour. The daily walk. Or, like my three old ladies who are immobile, the voice they recognise, the hand they can hold, even the irritation of a long aching joint because the little grumble, the pain itself, is something tangible. We fear the unknown because it is unknown. Darkness seems absolute. This is the reason why so often old people leave their beds and potter about a room, searching for light. For clarity. Second childhood, yes, the same yearning for reassurance that small children cry for, whimpering from a cot. Yet not so easily assuaged. For the old have known life, have known mobility, strength, friendship, love, and hatred too perhaps, and enmity. Even an angry word at midnight now could awake intelligence to action, send the blood coursing through tired veins. But they are alone, with the basic self, and the knowledge of this, and all that has gone before, demands new courage. When I last saw Shirley, just before Christmas, she greeted me with even greater warmth than before when I bent to kiss her. 'I've made a great plan', she told me, 'I'm not going to sit doing nothing here all day, or just listening to my transistor radio. And if I am with the rest of them in the lounge they fall asleep. It's not good enough'.

'So what?' I asked her.

'Well,' she said, 'I want to do something constructive. I know you are not a church-goer, but being creative, with your books, you'll understand. I believe in the power of thought, and the power of prayer. And when I am here alone, in my room, I'm going to think of all the people in the world who are unhappy or sick, and I'm going to pray for them. It will work like my radio here. The thought, the prayer, will somehow reach them. So, dear, just make a list of anyone you know who is ill or miserable, and when you next come, tell me their names, and I'll add them to the number'.

As I drove away from the Old People's Home I thought of several who might benefit from Shirley's therapy, but most of all, perhaps, she had found the answer to loneliness within herself. Just as Skip at ninety-one chops wood and fights decay, so Shirley will triumph over shadows through the months that lie ahead. Both share a firm faith in God and the hereafter, but the message is one that can be grasped by all, believer and non-believer alike.

'To grow old is more difficult than to die'. says Amiel's Journal, 'but to know *how* to grow old is the master-work of wisdom'.

Yes, and more than this besides, to face death, if we can, with equanimity. To live our lives each day as though we were to live forever, yet not forgetting that each day may be our last.

Mrs S. I. Goldsmith (aged 93)

I have just written a book on my life and am calling it 'Ninety Years Young'.

I have had a most interesting life chiefly because I have always taken an interest in everything and also in people. I am sure that helps to keep one young.

So many old people get wrapped up in themselves and their own concerns and worry about their health etc; worry does no good in any way and only depresses people. I do not think one should be continually looking for attention and sympathy. One dear old friend who died when she was over eighty, told me one should always make friends with the younger generations. When she died she had over three hundred at her funeral which took place in a blizzard one day in April.

Numbers of the present younger generations are not interested in old people but they should remember that the day will come when they will also be old and want friends.

I think friendship and interest in others helps to keep one young. I am also a great one for a good night's sleep and have never kept continuous late nights. One good tip is thirty-six hours' rest a month. I know several women who continually did this in India and kept fit and we all know that Sir Winston Churchill believed in his afternoon's rest.

Sir Paul Grey

KCMG. Diplomat. Minister to Prussia, 1951–54. Ambassador to Czechoslovakia, 1957–60. Ambassador to Switzerland, 1960–64.

How little has been written about old age and death! About growing old, yes; and about dying, and especially about the young dying:

> Brightness falls from the air
> queens have died young and fair
> Dust hath closed Helen's eye.

But not about old age, as the time for reassembling the forces of life, nor, except by some of the philosophers, and in the great scriptural passages, about death the dark angel, who comes to relieve those who stand guard over the fortress of life.

Death, after all, is the culmination of a life which, long or short, is always a unity. And death is only fearful if life is fearful. Tragic, yes: awful, yes. But not horrible, or to be shrouded in euphemism or secrecy, or to be swept aside as best not talked about. The real sorrow is that so many of us have lost our joy in life. We watch death at work among ourselves and our friends, and are obsessed by the thought of whole regions and civilisations dying, of the earth shrivelling and the seas no longer washing the shores. The glorious figure of Adam which Michelangelo created for us is forgotten and replaced by a gloomy anatomical figure. Science, and our own restless minds, which once offered us so bright a future, have torn our unity to shreds and left us with only ourselves for company – and that, as we all know, is poor company indeed.

Yet, if it be a virtue to have felt and to have known much, our generation has been most fortunate and should be most thankful. We have endured something. We have passed some, at least, of the tests. We have seen great changes; much that needed change, much that has proved none the better for it.

Many of our isms have become wasms, as an old friend said to me when Molotov signed his pact with Ribbentrop. We have fought tyrants and been present at their deaths. And we can also look back to an older England – to a time when, at least in the thinking of some of us, our country was gayer, more good humoured, more boyish and more united than she appears to be today; when the scale seemed different, when there were still giants walking the land.

And each of us has his memories. The sight of a young girl picking flowers in an island garden, by the sea. The sound of guns across the Channel, and the sudden knowledge that one's country was a living and a sacred thing, most dear because most vulnerable, as all love is vulnerable. The sadness of old battlefields when the fighting is over; the desolation of the land and of the sea, so full of the unknown dead. The sound of a song, half-forgotten and which no-one sings any more – '*un vecchio ritornello che nessuno canta piu*'. And, above and through all these things, the feeling that men and women had gathered together for a great battle, and that it was good to be alive and to have been with them.

But we seldom know how much of the past is over and done with, and how much still lives. Perhaps we keep some of it to ourselves more from fear of how it will be received than from doubt of its validity. And much remains uncertain. Dreams can be false counsellors, flattering us about the parts we have played: 'In sleep a King, but waking no such matter'.

So, in the end, the truth guards its secret. '*Tout passe, tout casse, tout lasse*'. But, if we tread the *via dolorosa* without discovering its meaning, we forget the glad, confident morning of others and the blessed light which shines equally on them and on us. God knows that we have reason to fear for the people and the things we love. The young are so vulnerable, and things are quite defenceless. But the young have no fear. They feel themselves imperishable, because they are full of that life which never has withdrawn itself, and never will withdraw itself from the human race. 'All appeared new and strange at first, inexpressibly rare and delightful and beautiful . . . Everything was at rest, free and immortal . . . Boys and girls tumbling in the streets, and playing, were moving jewels. I knew not that they were born or should die . . . The corn was orient and immortal wheat, which never should be reaped, nor was ever sown'. It is the morning of the world, which Rupert Brooke wrote of and which the young Gainsborough painted; the world which we re-enter in order to become young again:

O my Love, my love is young.
Age, I do defy thee.

Even we, who have known both the atomic bomb and the death camps, know how tenaciously all living things hold on to life, and how the light accompanies the darkness even to the edge of the abyss.

To suffer woes which Hope thinks infinite;
To forgive wrongs darker than death or night;
To defy Power, which seems omnipotent;
To love, and bear; to hope till Hope creates
From its own wreck the thing it contemplates.

If ever God was present, it was there, beside those poor, tormented creatures, whose cries will accompany some of us to the day of our death. Like Prometheus, they suffered in order to deliver us from the old, cruel gods. For them, as Pericles said of his Athenians, the whole earth is a sepulchre. We cannot be sure that, in our day, the earth may not have to suffer a destruction even more absolute than any we have experienced. But we can, I think, be sure that, if it does, the spirit will go out to meet it and create, from the wreck of hope, something as durable as they achieved.

For they were the companions in battle of the men and women we knew, who went out of our lives in the last war, and whose pictures still stand on the desks of our friends, as young as when they left to meet whatever fate had in store for them. In the words with which an ambassador closes his despatch, we are, with great truth and respect, their most obedient and humble servants. They died, as a man should, '*debout et dans son rang*', as the old French knight said. So, when we come to the close, I hope we too may be strong enough to draw the sword and salute, as they did, the new presence; see the light run along the blade, feel the clash of steel upon steel, and know that we have met the last of our enemies.

'*On ne peut ni trop braver les hommes, ni trop s'humilier devant Dieu*'. It would be wrong, in writing of either age or death, to ignore the hope that has accompanied so many men and women as wise, as gay and as valiant as any of our countrymen: that all whom they have loved and who have been their companions will, in some fashion, greet them again; that they will see sights, and hear sounds too, like the trumpets which Bunyan imagined sounding for them on the other side; and that the angels will come out to meet them on their passage.

But no religion is of any use unless it meets, not only the imagination of youth, but the experience of age. Our generation has sown the wind and reaped the whirlwind. It has seen the worm in the bud. It has witnessed the power which lives in a single atom, and knows that such a power is only an infinitesimal fraction of the power which holds the universe together. It knows, therefore, that the love which moves the sun and the other stars is also terrible as an army with banners.

But we are given a respite after a storm. If we look at our friends, we see that the day-star returns to them in the evening, to give light when the day itself declines; that Lucifer, son of the morning, who fell from heaven, gives way to

Lucifer the true light-bearer – '*ille, inquam, Lucifer qui nescit occasum*'.

'Holy is the true Light, and most wonderful, giving radiance to them that endured in the heat of conflict. From Christ they inherit a home of unfailing splendour, in which they will rejoice with gladness evermore'.

Harman Grisewood

CBE. Chief Assistant to the Director-General BBC, 1955-64. King Christian X Freedom Medal, 1946. Author.

The past has left us a rich literature of death, but a very meagre literature of old age. The discrepancy would be no more than an oddity of history were it not that nowadays old age needs all the moral support it can get, from the arts or from anywhere else. A succession of great masterpieces has surely done justice to every aspect of death. But old age comes to us undernourished by the world's thinkers and writers. It is indeed so little regarded now that it is in danger of losing its identity.

Old age is in danger from those who pretend to ignore it by all manner of disguises. Some are pleasantly deceptive, while others are ludicrous failures, but they are all harmful to the merits of old age by wishing it away as if it were an evil plague. It is also in danger from its professional organ-isers, who tranquillise it into immobility by drugs or tele-vision. And it is in mortal danger from those who would deal with it by extermination – the euthanasiasts.

Of course there are famous literary portraits of old age, and no lack of splendid canvasses. But most of these are laments for a lost youth. What is wanting is a convincing portrayal of the advantages of being old. Christians who still use the psalter pray to a God 'who gives joy to my youth'. There are no hymns for old age. The ancient pagans made no paeans of thankfulness for length of years. The lyre had no music for the days of serenity and reflection. The Christians who have succeeded so well with death seem to have failed with senescence.

The heroes of the Christian religion, it is true, have given us a variety of noble examples which we may read about in the lives of the long-lived saints. The failure has been in popular communication. When attempts are made to popularise the message of these venerable figures often the result is too close to the Stoic pattern for anything identifiably Christian to emerge. We are left with mournful platitudes like those of Marcus Aurelius – variations on the theme of endurance. But we should not despair. Remembering how many changes of emphasis have occurred in the development of Christian piety, and how many discoveries have been made in response to new needs, we may be encouraged to believe that the time has come for us to bring to light those special qualities in old age which have lain neglected these many centuries. Now is surely the time, when more and more people are living longer and longer. Now is the time, for medicine has given us a greater concealment to infirmity. And the time must be now because unless we do discover some conspicuous merit in being old, the exterminationists will have their way with us.

I can remember only one speech which praised old age above other earthly states. Desmond MacCarthy was the spokesman for the friends of Sir Max Beerbohm who had met together to celebrate his seventieth birthday. Desmond delighted his audience by declaring that the Gods had conferred upon Max at his birth their own most precious gift – eternal old age. Until he died at eighty-four, Max Beerbohm continued to show his visitors the companionable attractions of an enviable old age. There could be no thought of pity towards one so happy in the practice of virtues that take a lifetime to perfect. He received you with a courtesy which no younger person could imitate. He made you feel at ease with a subtlety wrought by years of sensitive understanding. His talk of people and events conveyed a reality which only reflection could bring. Above all there was a pervasive charity surrounding like a nimbus his sharpest criticism of those he had reason to deride. You left him feeling quite sure that 'ripeness is all'.

The bitterness of old age is not at having made mistakes however grievous, but in failing to have equipped oneself with enough eagerness for life. If you reach seventy with no lively enjoyment of other people for their own sakes, you will soon fall out with everyone around you for failing to bring you the satisfaction which once you could get for yourself. If you have looked out upon the world chiefly as a source of gratification, you will growingly reproach it for having lost the only point it had. Zest brings insight. Insight brings love. And love brings an independence from circumstance and a freedom from time itself. It is late at seventy to start those major alterations within oneself which are necessary for ripening the fruits of old age. But the attempt must be made. The required husbandry includes a compassion for the world which exceeds all expectations from it. The disposition of things seems to be that you must love the world before you are fit to leave it.

St Paul gives us a clue to the secret of a fruitful old age in a semi-soliloquy which he passed on in writing to the Phillipians. 'Death is a prize to be won', he wrote, 'But what if living on in this mortal body is the only way to harvest what I have sown?'

Not only for the great apostle but for all of us, old age is a harvest and we must live on in this mortal body waiting for the reaper. For some, as it was for Max, it is a harvest festival. It can be festive for anyone who takes the trouble to offer the fruits in a suitable arrangement. There are as many ways of decking out a church as there are harvests to bring home. But it is the celebration which is the point most often missed.

The celebration is for a lifetime of experience not one item of which is complete without some element of recollection. And it is the recollection which gives the meaning. It is the meaning which brings the rejoicing. The lifetime of experience is not over at any particular age. You can make it brimful of meaning at any time. There can be new departures at any age. The oldest person on earth is in fact just starting upon the plenitude of life.

D.J. Hall

Poet and novelist.

When I was a child I often enjoyed imagining my death, usually when I had behaved badly and knew it, or when I had been accused of wrong-doing when I was innocent: I saw my parents and friends finding me, beautiful in death as in life, and being filled with remorse, while I looking down on them recognized that my death was a noble atonement for whatever I had or had not committed. In my adolescence, when my fancies roamed the whole world for fields to conquer, when I sorrowed for the brevity of love and of beauty, and of the unhappiness of mankind in the midst of such wonder of creation; when I wrote passionate and very bad poetry and longed to create something that would change the lot of man from sadness to joy; then, too, I thought of death. Especially in the spring, when the sap was rising not only in the trees but in me; it would be beautiful to die at the very moment of creation, though it would be sad to die before my genius had flowered, and of course been recognized – though this after-thought was a little vulgar. There came, too, the exquisite pain of unrequited love. I was continually in love, and when I was deceived – oh, death come soon, come quickly, and my love shall mourn her loss.

Such thoughts and emotions can be no more original than any others that I may record; death has been a subject fascinating to men and women for so long that it is inconceivable that any aspect of it has been left unexplored; yet every human being is an unique creation; and as such I must speak, since the variations within the similarities are infinite.

My pleasure in dramatising the prospect of my death came largely from my death being so unlikely. However much a young man may pretend even to a horror of death, his fear is of something which if he is healthy he knows in his bones to be remote, save for an unforeseeable accident. I was exceedingly healthy and strong. So, through the years my thoughts and emotions progressed from the early morbid preoccupation to the dramatic, to the romantic, coming at ever-widening intervals and with diminishing enjoyment until at the age of twenty-four I married a young woman with whom I have never been happier than we are now after forty-six years. In such a marriage one does not think of death. However improbable my youthful decease might still be, to dwell on it could no longer be a fantasy since my new responsibility for a loved human being was a reality. Death was not to be imagined.

When I was twenty-eight I met a man who set me a lifelong example: Scott Macfie, a remarkable linguist, authority on Romani, a musician, writer, traveller, soldier, friend to many great figures in the arts and at one time rich. When on a winter's evening I came to his farmhouse high above Wensleydale he was old, knew that he was dying, almost all his friends were dead, he had no family and had lost most of his money, mainly through lack of interest in it. Outwardly, he had little left for which most people would wish to live. Although under doctor's orders not to tire himself, he talked to me with few breaks for three days during which he revealed himself to be the most complete man and the happiest I have ever met; and this was because he had never let slip any opportunity for new experience which might increase his understanding, especially of people. He had gathered such a store as would have sustained several lifetimes, yet he was in himself so young that I was unaware of any disparity in age. When he spoke of death, it was of yet another experience

65

– you never knew what might turn up. What an example for a young man to add to his natural optimism!

Thoughts of death, as I knew in my youth, have for me little to do with fear of it. Although before the war I adventured quite a lot in foreign countries and among some very strange people, my wife often with me, we did not fear what could easily have come to us. Fear came with the war, I think partly because of anger: the obvious danger of death from a bomb in London terrified me because I was furious at its senselessness. Anger and fear are closely linked, and anger tends to make me frightened because it is usually ugly and shameful even when it is 'righteous', while fear in its turn makes me angry, I suppose from shame at a weakness; the interaction of the two can produce mounting horror in me. On the other hand when I was quite on my own in eastern Europe as far as the Dniester, where the danger was of a subtler kind, I felt no fear at all. I think this was partly due to a return of my world of fantasy which grew to embrace everything I did until the war was over. What I did may or may not have been useful and sensible, but I did it in the third person; I, myself, looked at this person doing improbable things, deploring, admiring, sometimes anxious for him but rarely frightened because it could never be really me. Everyone of course lives to some extent in a world created by himself, and some people would find life intolerable without this protection which is inclined to grow more necessary to them with age, even though fantasy, having no boundaries, may lead to doubts about the reality of anything, including oneself.

What, then, do I feel about old age and death now that I am seventy, if you can call that old? Truly, I neither think nor feel much about either. My sense of fantasy is no less strong, but I have it under control; I am no longer fooled by it and use it consciously to amuse. I have an irregular heart which prevents my running and makes me puff going up hills but which I am told is unlikely to kill me: I have always raced up and down stairs and done everything at top speed, except in the intervals of doing absolutely nothing, so although I have adapted my pace I sometimes chafe because the older I become the more I know how much there is to learn and to see, and there simply is not going to be time to discover a little of what I seek, not to mention looking into my own particular store to find out what it means and if there is anything worthwhile to pass on. My mind is too much filled with other things to think often about how old I am.

Rare, too, is my consideration of death; and, yes, perhaps here I do retain some fantasy. I have never since childhood taken seriously the likelihood of my death and still find it hard to do so when the course of nature makes it far nearer and the man-made hazards are immensely greater. The other day by almost incredible good fortune, after my car had just been overhauled, a service station mechanic saw that my steering coupling was broken: a moment before or after, it could have parted and I should have been dead, and perhaps several others with me. The coupling was replaced, and a few days later when I was driving on a motorway the shock of the discovery remained such that I had to dismiss – as most unsuitable in such a place – the thought that perhaps I had indeed died, that the coupling had parted and that I had driven on and was still driving in another life, invisible to those around me.

Here there was a fantasy within a fantasy because of the vision of a life after death. Unless, in the Christian or other religious sense, you are an unquestioning believer in immortality, any other kind of belief or hope for it is bound to be speculative: it may seem absurd to suppose that anything so aesthetically detailed in form, colour and design as our world and its myriad beasts, fishes, flowers and insects, capped by the appearance of mankind and its psyche just happened; but there is not much evidence, and certainly no proof, that a Great Mind or Life Force was at work giving each man and woman an immortal soul. On the other hand only the rather old-fashioned rationalists continue to dismiss the possibility, and few scientists of any stature are prepared any longer wholly to ignore it.

I have listened over the years to countless arguments for and against a future life and now I do not know what I think, because my only anxiety about death is that my wife and I should go together, and that is not really an anxiety about death but about the manner of dying and an almost unimaginable kind of living: if I should enter another life we might not be together, and I should not like that life. This world, with all its faults and the imbecilities of its inhabitants, I still find beautiful, intellectually stimulating and physically exciting. Some might say that I am influenced in my attitude by having been born under Leo, and that brings in yet another imponderable which some people are not even prepared to discuss. But imponderables, whether they amuse, alarm, please or mystify, are what really matter since the desire to pursue them has been the spur of every man from the beginning in his difficult search for the good life.

Meanwhile, I continue to agree with William Blake that 'Everything possible to be believ'd is an image of truth'.

Manya Harari

Writer, publisher. Republished from 'Manya Harari, Memoirs, 1960–1969' (Harvill Press, London, 1972).

. . . The diagnosis was a severe form of cancer. On learning this she wrote the following letter to her son.

'I am writing because I want you to know how I feel about being ill.

'Firstly, as I told you, it is no way a shocking surprise, because I have known it for a long time; not, of course, in any clear way but so well, however unclearly, that I would have been more surprised to find that there was nothing the matter with me. This has spared me the difficulty of sudden adjustment. It also means that what I now think has not been thought up on the spur of the moment.

'Secondly, I do not think death a desirable thing, so you can be quite sure that I'll do everything I can to put it off. I know that, as you say, there are various things nowadays one can do and I had a good practical talk with Gordon Bourne. He told me that in my particular case there is a very good chance of the ray treatment not only arresting the spread of the disease but actually dissolving (whatever the word is) this particular lump, and also that there are other chemical methods of treatment as well, if this one fails. Naturally, he did not pretend that any of it was a panacea, or that one can say with certainty what would succeed or for how long. I am telling you this not out of a morbid rejection of optimism but because it is obviously true, and also because of what I want to say next.

'There are two things that help me to see things in proportion. One is that being ill and dying is a job, in a sense like any other, but of course an important one. The important thing is to do it as well as one can. I find that knowing about it in advance, however uncertain the date, but with a knowledge more precise than one has when one is well is something so real, factual and also demanding, that it leaves one hardly any room for nostalgia or sadness for oneself, or even for regretting what one hasn't managed to get done in life. I feel this has become entirely God's business to look after: all there is to do is to get on with making good sense of what there is ahead. When I talk of 'making as good a job of it as one can' I don't of course mean doing anything special like, say, withdrawing mentally into some special place. I only mean living more attentively than I have been in the habit of doing. This at present seems to be something very simple – I don't mean easy, but uncomplicated. In this sense, having some advance knowledge makes things simpler because it brings them into focus, and is therefore a considerable help – at least I feel it is to me.

'The other thing, which is very closely linked up with this is my view of death in general. I don't think the difference between your philosophy and mine need make it difficult for us to understand each other about it. The relevant point about mine is that death is a mystery at least as great as life. As I am sure you will understand, what I mean is that, for me, death has none of the element of tragic futility which it has for many other people. It is not somewhere 'out there ' – it is properly within the same order as life and (however little enthusiasm one may have for it) to be viewed as eminently normal and, like life, with a certain piety. Further than that, the "consolations of religion" are very solid and very great. The reason I talk so much about what I feel is that I think it will help us both if we know it. But, of course, I have said nothing about my distress for others. I know, darling, that you do and will feel sad, and that nothing I can say will prevent this. Only do remember that it is normal for one to survive one's parents; and I do know from experience that when it happens, one does accept it – one's whole nature is geared to accepting it – and somehow one feels more, not less rooted in life because one is more strongly linked to the generation before one. This is no disrespect to one's parents; on the contrary, it is simply in the nature of things.

'I needn't tell you that the real problem for me is Ralph. The doctor has promised not to tell him sooner than is necessary. Then, we'll see: I can only hope for some miracle to make it more acceptable to him than it would be now. Anyhow, one can't work everything out in advance'.

In order to spare Ralph the unhappiness of knowing that she was in danger, she continued to live as nearly normal a life as was possible . . . Eventually she entered a clinic for treatment but had only been there a few days when Ralph became seriously ill. She at once came out and nursed him for the few days he still had to live.

When later . . . she was told that she had only a few weeks before her, she made no mention of this or of the fact that she had received the Last Sacraments, but ordered champagne all round . . . Even if she had not told a friend: 'I am infinitely happy and only sad that I am too weak to share my happiness' it was plain that she was at peace. Nor did she lose her sense of humour. To someone who had been praying until recently for her recovery and had now changed her intention, but had certainly never made any mention of this, she remarked: 'Thank goodness, you look quite different since you have stopped telling God what to do about me'.

When she first knew that she was seriously ill, she had written to her son, 'Dying is a job . . . the important thing is to do it as well as one can'. When death was imminent her attitude was the same.

Two days before she died, she looked for the first time troubled and said: 'Until now I have always known what God wanted me to do, but now I feel quite extraordinary, and I am not sure what to do. Do you think the cancer has reached my brain?'

When told that she was actually dying and that it would

not last long, she relaxed and said: 'In that case it is very simple, but would it be peculiar if I asked to have the Last Sacraments again?'

L. P. Hartley

CBE. Companion of Literature. James Tait Black Memorial Prize, 1947; W. H. Heinemann Foundation Award, 1953. Author and critic. Notes written shortly before he died and edited by R.R.

The problem of old age – if it is a problem – is not so different from the phenomenon of death as might immediately appear. The one is a gradual preparation for the other, except in the case of sudden death, of which our age has had only too many examples. The subject is almost too solemn to write about. What can one say of something from which most sufferers either turn away, or do not wish to hear, or feel it is in bad taste to mention it at all? Yet most people have had to undergo it, or their friends have. They may take it more lightheartedly, as they do to-day, but with most people there is a pang when the church door or the crematorium closes.

There are other folk who do (not) dread the thought of death, and even welcome old age as a prelude to it. I cannot understand that, but one can observe, among the animals, especially among cats, that they do not struggle against their fate of illness, they give way to it, they accept it with a certain dignity, and retire to wherever it may be, to die alone.

Do we live in a happier condition than the animals, who take what they feel is coming to them for granted, and in some cases resist any efforts to cure them, knowing that their time has come?

We, being more sensitive than they, and more fearful for our future in the next world are either indifferent to (death), or welcome it as a release from suffering, or simply as the oblivion which many people desire. On the other hand, I have been told there is a physical preparation for death which makes it less awful and after a long illness in old age, almost welcome. Not only suicides are made this way, but men and women who feel they can bear no longer the torments of the flesh, and would be glad to give them up.

'How wonderful is death,/Death and his brother sleep', wrote Shelley, and no one who has suffered from the long dark hours of insomnia would deny the second. But death – the universal negative – how does it link up with old age?

Shelley was a young man when he died that tragic death; but did he really cling to life? Was not life to him a continuation of age, not old, for I doubt if he ever thought of himself as old . . . but as someone whom age could not wither or custom stale. One does not think of him as belonging to old age, or even to death, though he seems to have chosen it, but as an immortal being, deathless, as he was lifeless. Old age could not touch him.

Perhaps this is true of many artists, to whom old age is not a wasting but a continuance and forward looking of their powers, as it was with Michelangelo and Verdi and Tolstoy and Titian, for instance, who achieved many of their great works at an advanced age, and who were not haunted, or affected, by the idea of old age.

Cum veniet tacito
Curva senecta pede.

But of course, sadly enough, there are far more examples to the contrary – of 'whom the gods love die young'. Many people (I did myself) feel themselves immortal until a certain age – whatever that may be – three score years and ten – and after that may be haunted by the thought of death, and what they have done, and what they have not done. Perhaps Shelley's lines, 'How wonderful is death . . .' do afford a certain concord, if only from the use of the word 'wonderful', which is equally true of life and death. 'As for my life', said the young Sir Thomas Browne, 'it is a miracle of thirty years'. Wonderful! Wonderful! And again later, 'The long habit of living indisposeth us for dying'. His mind was set on the next world. I don't know how old he lived to be, but he was obviously not afraid of death – he welcomed it, as the last chapter of *Urn Burial*, with its glorious paragraphs about the future world shows: '*Pyramids, Arches, Obelisks,* were but the irregularities of vain-glory, and wilde enormities of ancient magnanimity. But the most magnanimous resolution rests in the Christian Religion, which trampleth upon pride, and sits on the neck of ambition, humbly pursuing that infallible perpetuity, unto which all others must diminish their diameters, and be poorly seen in the Angles of contingency . . . (*Angulus contingentia,* the least of all Angles). "Tis all one to lye in St *Innocent's* Churchyard (*in Paris,* where bodies soon consume) as in the sands of Ægypt: Ready to be anything, in the ecstasie of being ever, and as content with six foot as the Mole of *Adrianus* (a stately *Mausoleum* or sepulchral pyle, built by *Adrianus* in *Rome,* where now standeth the Castle of St *Angelo*).

Rosemary Haughton

Writer, lecturer, broadcaster.

There is a game, called 'Musical Parcel', much played at parties for small children. A huge, bulky parcel, tied up with much string, is passed from hand to hand round the circle of children, while music plays. But when the music stops, the child who finds himself holding the parcel begins feverishly to unwrap it, pulling at the knots, tearing recklessly at the paper, or patiently finding the best ways to open it up. Then the music begins again, and the parcel continues its journey until it stops once more and another excited child wrestles with the wrappings. So it goes on, and it goes on a long time, because the outer wrapping, when at last removed, reveals only more paper, more string, of a different colour perhaps, and beneath that yet another layer, and another, and another. As the parcel sheds its layers the floor around is littered with cast off wrappings and the excitement mounts. For the smaller the fast-travelling parcel becomes the greater the hope that, at last, one will be able to come at the prize, the little, precious thing at the heart of all the layers of wrapping. What will it be like? Who will get it?

Perhaps it seems strange to describe a children's party game when death and old age are the subject, but this game provides an excellent image of the Christian theology of death. Death is the final unwrapping, the revelation of what each human being truly is, when all earthly things are stripped away. And the wrappings? They are what St Paul called 'the flesh', that much misunderstood phrase which simply means the state of the human being, body and soul, cut off from knowledge of God and so of himself, isolated with his fears and suspicions and protectives devices, both personal and communal.

Each child born into the world is a person, a life packed with boundless possibilities of beauty and love, capable of glory, 'made in God's image', yet, from the moment of birth and even before, the influences begin that wrap him or her in thick layers of 'the flesh'. The physical helplessness of the infant, his need for reassurance, his vulnerability to every nuance of mood in those who care (or don't care) for him – these things already *require* him to protect himself and survive as he can, by aggressive cries, by (very quickly) learning to provoke reactions of pity or attention and to provide food. As he grows, he learns - again *necessarily* – to manipulate those around him for his own needs. He creates fantasies to comfort himself and compensate for the fear his helplessness and ignorance engenders. To survive, he must consider his own needs, and how to use others to satisfy them. So the layers of the life of the flesh are wrapped around him, and as time goes on he is tied up, by himself and by others, in the complicated knots of social obligation and cultural expectation which his particular group has devised, over the generations, to make life reasonably secure and stable, if not very happy. By the time he is adult he is so securely tied up that he can't imagine himself as anything but this particular parcel.

Yet, all the time, from the beginning, as the rhythm of life quickens and he goes from hand to hand, the human parcel has a curious conviction that there is something more. A loving touch, a moment of intimacy, a simple pleasure that yet seems to mean more than the momentary satisfaction – such things make the human being desire, obscurely, to know what lies within himself. He is not content to know only his exterior wrappings, however handsome and well tied they may be.

But in his desire to discover himself he cannot act alone. It is always *another* hand that fumbles at the knots, pulls off the paper. It may be a loving hand that helps to reveal something a little nearer the heart of the matter. Or it may be a cruel, unthinking hand, or the grip of the rapacious, wanting to possess whatever treasure lies within. Sometimes the parcel resists, throwing himself once more in the on-rush of daily life, amusement, career, to escape the attempt to probe the reality under all the layers. There are people who seem never to stop the music long enough to be real at all.

But, God willing, the human parcel keeps, however painfully and unknowingly, the desire for truth which makes him co-operate with the hands that pull and twitch at the next layer. For the Christian, the teaching is explicit: in order to know God, at the heart of the Self, it is necessary to be vulnerable to the needs and demands of others, to give, to be open. The music goes on, there are necessary routines and work to be done, but the process of unwrapping goes on too.

Sometimes you can see it happening very fast. A great experience of love, or pain, can remove so many layers that the spirit seems almost to be free – or at least one can see it shining through the remaining layers. Saints, as they grow, show to others that it is possible to live with very few wrappings. But for most of us, we cling to our wrappings, they are torn from us against our will. They are beautiful, after all. They consist, among other things, of health and beauty and friendship and talent. We don't want to leave these behind, and indeed we cannot do so wilfully, for the parcel cannot unwrap *itself*. So, for most of us, the hand of God comes to help us, and gently but firmly removes from us those wrappings that we thought most important to us. And, if we have tried to co-operate, however feebly, with the earlier stages of our life's game of musical parcel, we find that ageing is not, after all, the process of losing what made life worth living, but of shedding, gradually and even contentedly, the things (often good in themselves) that distracted us from the search for the truth of ourselves.

It isn't always so. The suspicious and bitter, who have

never been open to love and hope, remain resistant, fighting against the inevitable, blaming relations, fate, God, the doctor, or the government for everything that goes wrong. And sometimes real hardships and loneliness makes it almost impossible to do more than hang on to the vestiges of life, and wait. Here again, it depends on others who can, by their affection and concern, make it easier to accept the last stripping of the fading flesh. It is always another hand that is needed, and the importance of the last years has been clear to all truly human cultures. 'Honour thy father and thy mother' was not a command merely for the sake of security of inheritance and maintenance of property, it was also a command to respect the great work of God in the weakened years of those who had once been the strong ones. A culture that forgets this command is one that, inevitably, encourages everyone in it at any age to *preserve* his protective wrappings and not to be open to what life brings, for in such a culture it brings most often jealousy and fear and competition, the mastery of the strong and suppression of the poor and weak.

The last enemy is death. But he is only enemy to the final wrappings of the flesh. His is often a rough and ruthless hand, but not a fearful one to those who have allowed it already to remove all but the transparent veil that conceals reality. Death, in scripture, is not merely the moment of physical dying, but the influence throughout life that destroys man's fleshly self-confidence: illness, sorrow, fear, reaching out long arms from the dark grave to clutch at the ankles of men walking in daylight. So the final act of dying is only the completion of many other acts of dying, stripping, liberation.

But for many, the finality and inevitabilty of it has an effect that earlier 'dyings' had not had. Sometimes, those who have thus far evaded the meaning of those moments in life that are able to strip off the hampering layers of the flesh, realise at the last what it is all about. People working with the dying are familiar with this process, as the rebellious and frightened come to terms with death, relax, even smile, and prepare quietly and lovingly to leave behind what had once seemed so impossbile to part with. The experience of dying is the greatest unwrapping, the great liberation, and it can also be an important moment of unwrapping, for the relatives and friends who share it and help it. They learn, seeing it, to face their own mortality and to recognize it not as a horror to be pushed out of mind, but as an opportunity to be awaited and prepared for.

We don't know, we can't guess, what we shall find when the last wrappings are removed.

A recurring theme in fairy tales is that the enchanted prince, condemned by an evil spell to the form of some hideous animal or wizened crone, is revealed in his true shape at last, when the love of the heroine has triumphed over pain and trouble to bring him the water of life, or the kiss that means peace and union. Sometimes it is the princess, horribly disguised, who is set free by the hero's devotion. In such ways, the folk lore of all times and places bears witness in lucid symbols to the reality which was finally displayed when Christ rose from the dead. He became, in himself, both the promise and the fact of eternal life, to be revealed when earthly music ceases, and we discover in the silence of God the truth and the wholeness and the harmony.

The Rt Rev. Trevor Huddleston

DD. *Bishop of Stepney (since 1968); Bishop of Masasi (1960-68).*
Author. A sermon preached for 'Help the Aged' at St Martin-in-the
Fields.

The first reason why we are here this afternoon – the reason
why we are in church at all – is that we recognise our need
to give thanks. And we give thanks not to each other: not to
the great British public: not even to our own faithful sub-
scribers – but to God. We make our own that most marvellous verse in the Epistle of St James: 'All good giving, every
perfect gift, comes from above, from the Father of the lights
of heaven. With him there is no variation, no play of passing
shadows'.

We are here because we want to thank 'the Father of the
lights of heaven' for one of the greatest of all his gifts: *old
age*. And, more especially, for the presence amongst us, in
our society, everywhere, of those whom we call the old, the
elderly, the aged: but whom no abstract definition can ad-
equately define at all.

And the whole theme of my address this afternoon is going
to be one of thanksgiving – if only because I recognise how
much, in my own life, I owe to friends who were old in
years when I was young. I mean really old: but I also mean,
in another sense, so completely and beautifully human, wise
and loving that their age (in years) meant and means nothing.
And if I had to extract a quality or a virtue common to them
all, I should have no difficulty. It is *joy*. Like that of Martha,
an old African woman, blind, and living in one squalid room
in a back street of Sophiatown, Johannesburg. Living in utter
poverty. I can see her now and hear the sound of her stick

tapping the pavement as she walked slowly up the hill to church, sometimes at 5.30 in the morning: always at least an hour before the Eucharist so that she would have time to pray. But above all I can see her smile. Or another old African lady, Julia, who taught me in one sentence the meaning of God's loving providence because the whole of her life was evidence that she believed it. 'Remember', she said, when one of us young clergy was fussing and fretting about a scheme that had gone wrong or a service that hadn't gone right – 'Remember - God minds his own business'.

Or that old man on the Makonda plateau in Southern Tanzania, whose name I have forgotten, but whom I confirmed on a bitterly cold, windy morning. I had felt frozen under three blankets in a warm hut: he was in a single, thread-bare blanket and the walls of his hut were full of holes and he was alone. But the laying on of hands in confirmation meant more to him than any gift I could have brought him and his whole face was radiant . . . And so I could go on.

The old, the wise, the beautiful, the good . . . gifts 'from the Father of the lights of heaven – with whom (AV) is no variableness or shadow of turning' – and who, each single blessed one of them – has enriched my life beyond measure because they have brought into it the meaning of joy as it is in God himself – stemming from, a real part of his own changelessness.

It is really an astonishing thing that a civilisation like ours – drawing all its positive value from the great Hebrew-Christian tradition should have so largely forgotten what that tradition says about old age.

How, in fact, the blessing of God himself is seen to consist in length of days. The patriarchs of the Old Testament, 'the friends of God', Abraham, Isaac, Joseph are all represented as 'of good old age . . . full of years'.

The fear of the Lord', says the writer of Proverbs, 'is the beginning of wisdom . . . For by me your days will be multiplied and years will be added to your life'.

In thy strength the King rejoices, O Lord,
and in thy help how greatly he exults,
He asked life of thee; thou gavest it to him,
length of days for ever and ever.
With *long life* I will satisfy him
and show him my salvation.

And when God enters his world as the Babe of Bethlehem,
after the shepherds it is the Magi – the wise old men from
the East who first came to worship him: it is Simeon, the
old man 'upright and devout' who takes him in his arms and
prophesies: it is Anna, 'a very old woman', who tells about
the child to all who were looking for the liberation of
Jerusalem.

Old age is a blessing – not a curse – in the Scripture. Why
does it sound like special pleading to talk of it thus today?
Are God's blessings so changed that they can no longer be
reckoned in the old currency? Or is our currency so changed
that we have forgotten the purpose of God for man – as man?
Is the fact that we categorise 'the young' and 'the old' as the
problem areas of our social structure a judgment upon revealed religion? Or is it not more likely the judgment of God
that our society needs most to fear? I leave those questions
with you, and return to the theme of my address:
Thanksgiving.

And of course, we are here not only to thank God for the
gifts of old age and of the people who enshrine it. We are
here to thank God for another year of blessing on the societies
known as 'Help the Aged' or 'Voluntary and Christian
Service'.

But we all recognise that in an affluent society like our
own the fact that such effort is needed at all is a measure of
our misunderstanding of human priorities.

As Simone de Beauvoir so starkly puts it: 'What should a
society be, so that in his last years a man might still be a
man? The answer is simple: he would always have to have
been treated as a man. By the fate it allots to its members

who can no longer work, society gives itself away – it has always looked upon them as so much material. Society confesses that as far as it is concerned, profit is the only thing that counts, and that its "humanism" is mere window-dressing . . . Society cares about the individual only in so far as he is profitable. The young know this. Their anxiety as they enter in upon social life matches the anguish of the old as they are excluded from it'.

Simone de Beauvoir is not a Christian and her book *Old Age* is a fierce attack on the structures and meanings of capitalist society.

But it is a book with great insight and great compassion and great truth.

She quotes in her introduction the story of Buddha who, as Prince Siddartha, 'often escaped from the splendid palace in which his father kept him shut up and drove about the surrounding countryside. The first time he went out he saw a tottering, wrinkled, toothless, white-haired man, bowed, mumbling, and trembling as he propped himself along on his stick. The sight astonished the prince and the charioteer told him just what it meant to be old. 'It is the world's pity', cried Siddartha, 'that weak and ignorant beings, drunk with the vanity of youth, do not behold old age! Let us hurry back to the palace. What is the use of pleasures and delights, since I myself am the future dwelling-place of old age?'

But is that a cause for thanksgiving also?

I believe it is. Because I believe that truth – and especially poetic truth – is *always* a reason for thanksgiving.

'I myself am the future dwelling place of old age.' And what that means has recently been marvellously expressed by Phillip Larkin in 'The Old Fools': 'Perhaps being old is having lighted rooms. We shall find out.'

It is because old age *can* be the *truth* for all of us: *must* be the truth for most of us: that we must learn to love each other now.

Michael James Laws

Property maintenance consultant.

It is only during the last year or so that I have grudgingly accepted the fact that I am in middle age. Most of the time I tend to lose this number of years to escape it altogether, then just as I'm feeling good, up it pops on some official form or other. It seems society is bent on persistently reminding one of one's age. Either you are too young or too old.

From now on, as I approach old age, I treat the prospect with due respect and trepidation. Watching for the physical changes, hair losing its colour and thinning, the face more etched with lines conjured up from nowhere. The body slows down and muscles stiffen to the tread. Only the mind appears to stay its course. No, I do not particularly embrace old age but if I live through the middle years, I have no alternative. Good health at such a time will be a boon but there are no guarantees.

They say, only the good die young. Perhaps they are to be envied. For they miss the truly difficult path of living life at its most competitive, coming to terms with oneself. Possibly striving for a higher ideal, then when it is about in one's grasp only to be snatched away by an infirmity, old age or death. I have often thought that life itself is suffering and the brief intervals from such one's pleasure.

I imagine old age to be a sort of platform from which one prepares and contemplates with mind and soul for approaching death. From quite early in childhood I have been aware of dying. My feelings then, as now, vary from a numbed fear to complete equanimity. For it depends very much on mood. If content or happy I then tend to resent death. If I am serious or sad, then I accept it without question to be the logical conclusion.

Life then to me is very much like travelling on the Underground crossing London. I have passed the half-way station, Piccadilly Circus, and am well on my way to Cockfosters. I look behind at the tiny bright aperture that was my beginning, my birth. Not too far distant I see the end of the tunnel. The light is vague and hovers like a mirage. Time itself becomes the most precious value of all.

It is said in the *Bhagavad Gita*: Darma asks 'Of all the world's wonders, which is the most wonderful?' Yudhisthira replies: 'That no man, though he sees others dying all around him, believes that he himself will die'.

So what of everyone's personal dilemma? There is surely one consolation for us all. For the agnostic – total oblivion. For the believer – life after death and possible eventual paradise. Every man has a choice.

When my time comes I would like to be laid out on a balsa raft with fresh-cut coconut fronds festooned with sweet smelling tropical flowers. Gold-bodied maidens will wade into the lagoon and push me towards the warm trade winds of the Marquesas then, just as the great sun is about to sink below the horizon the bier is set alight by an arrow projected from the shore. As the raft, flowers, and I ignite, the sweet sound of tamoura bids me farewell as sparks and fire ricochet into the indigo heavens and the star-infested blue of night. When the rose-pink dawn arrives a solitary girl picks up all that remains of the farewell – a solitary limp-wet flower.

The Rt Hon the Earl of Longford, KG

Don, historian, author, politician, banker, publisher and philanthropist.

Cicero in *De Senectute* picks out four reasons why old age might appear to be unhappy. First it withdraws us from active pursuits; secondly it makes the body weaker; thirdly it deprives us of almost all physical pleasures and fourth it is not far-removed from death. He deals with each in turn whittling down the debit side and glorifying the assets of old age which, by the finish, is well in credit.

But first a word of definition or non-definition. Cicero's essay, the most famous ever written on the subject, was produced when he was sixty-two. The arguments are put into the mouth of the elder Cato, then supposedly eighty-four. In recent years Simone de Beauvoir points out in her comprehensive work on old age that 'as far as our own species is concerned old age is by no means easy to define' which indeed is obvious enough. Personally I am aware that life at sixty-two was one thing – life at sixty-seven (my present age) slightly different and if, by any chance one is spared so long, life at eighty-four will be something which one can't at present envisage. Some of us at sixty-seven are mistaken for fifty-seven, some for seventy-seven, so no general rules will apply very successfully. However, one must draw a line somewhere and for my purposes I begin old age at sixty-five. A male person of that age has no grounds for complaint if he is described as an old man or a female person as an old woman. Not that one likes to hear the former phrase applied to oneself or to see it written in print for the first time. In the course of a recent social enquiry I was photographed most respectably with two young women obtaining my autograph. One of them subsequently described me as 'a nice old man'. Mortifying but salutary. It is better than being described as 'a dirty old man', but it takes a little getting used to.

To keep referring to oneself as old or even elderly or ageing can become an embarrassment. Indeed all references to one's age are best eschewed wherever possible. Not long ago I remarked with intended humour: 'You know I am not more than a few years over seventy'. 'I suppose not', said my companion, too seriously for my liking. I shall not repeat that particular error. But everyone I should imagine is slightly pleased and flattered when he or she is taken to be younger than his actual age.

Yet would most of us if we had the chance put the clock back a few or many years? That I should think is highly doubtful. For many, perhaps for most people, the sheer fact of having lived a certain number of years is felt to be a kind of accomplishment irrespective of any particular achievement to be pointed to. The more satisfied one is with the results of one's labours whether in one's profession or the world of the family, the less likely one is to want to play the game over again. In old age with its reduced energies not a few of us are inclined to marvel at what we were capable of when we were younger. If at sixty-seven one were mistaken for sixty-two (if it happened) one would be hoping to get it both ways. The achievement such as it had been would still be 'in the bank' and at the same time one would be preening oneself on the greater youthfulness or lesser senility imputed.

Cicero argues that in old age although we are 'withdrawn from active pursuits' our chance of influence should be greater. In these latter days old age means retirement from a recognised profession other than that of solitary artist or thinker. In De Senectute Cato is made to say: 'I direct the Senate as to what wars should be waged and how'. Today such a role would be exceptional, though Sir Winston Churchill formed his last Cabinet at seventy-six. Lords Samuel and Pethick-Lawrence spoke up well in the Lords until the verge of ninety and Lord Brockway in his middle eighties is going stronger than ever. Normally retirement – whatever that may mean in the House of Lords – diminishes influence substantially, but scope is left for the individual who is freer to pursue the causes he most cares for when no longer inhibited by career requirements. Personally for good or for ill I became really well-known to the general public for the first time during our pornography inquiry. It came my way when I was sixty-five and could never have arisen if I had been still in the political rat-race.

Cicero admits that in old age one's strength diminishes but Cato says: 'I do not now feel the *need* of the strength of youth any more than when a young man I felt the need of the strength of the bull or the elephant'. One failing of the old, he concedes, which would not operate now. 'The orator', he writes, 'does lose in efficiency on account of old age because his success depends not only on his intellect but also upon his lungs and bodily strength'. With the coming of the microphone the old no longer suffer from this handicap as the examples just given illustrate. What he seems to underestimate is the increase of ailments and minor ill-health with advancing years. No doubt what Simone de Beauvoir says is relevant here. 'The age at which the decline begins has always depended upon the class to which a man belongs. The worker's decline begins earlier; its course is also far more rapid. During his years of "survival" his shattered body is the victim of disease and informity; whereas an elderly man who has had the good fortune of being able to look after his health may keep it more or less undamaged until his death'. And no doubt there are quite a number of men who have been over-working for years improve their health by retirement though others die off immediately. By and large in old age the body must be expected to be more rather than less of a nuisance.

Cicero devotes a good deal of his essay to discussing those

pleasures which decline with the years and those which become still more delightful. The weakening of the cruder passions he regards as pure gain: '. . . how blessed it is for the soul, after having, as it were, finished its campaigns of lust and ambition, of strife and enmity and of all the passions, to return within itself and, as the saying is "to live apart . . ." ' Old people may follow him here more readily than when he seems to take for granted a decline among the old of the pleasures of eating and drinking. Those who have attended many public banquets won't accept this for a moment.

The pleasures of conversation he singles out as greater than ever in old age. Personally I would find some parallel with the enchanting discussions one indulged in in one's student days. Perhaps what really stands in the way of good conversation is absorption in the day-to-day business of making a living and the selfishness inherent in the architecture of one's own career.

Cicero neglects on the one hand the fall in income that comes to most of us older people as our earning power diminishes. On the other hand, the ever-expanding and deepening joys of life in the family circle, if fortune is kind.

Finally, there is the approach of death which Lord Norwich (Duff-Cooper) called 'the time limit'. The uncertainty and the certainty are blended. Strictly speaking this is so throughout life. We know that we must all die sometime. In theory this might happen to any of us at any moment whatever our age. When I was in my middle fifties I took leave after lunch of my old Eton housemaster, C. M. Wells, then ninety-one. 'Good-bye Sir', I said and added, a shade patronisingly perhaps: 'I hope you'll keep well'. He pointed his hand at me with an old familiar gesture. 'I might die at any moment', he replied briskly, 'and so, my dear fellow, might you'. True enough at all times, but ever truer as one advances into old age. Even if one lives to be eighty, the next ten years will pass in a flash, as Malcolm Muggeridge said on his seventieth birthday recently. It is bad taste and boring to go round talking about death the whole time, but it must enter increasingly into all one's long-term planning, whether in a worldly or other-worldly sense.

Must the prospect of it be distinctly more depressing if one cannot believe in a better world to come than if one can? Cicero took a cheerful view of the whole matter. He believed in immortality, but had this to say about the opposite possibility: 'If I err in my belief that the souls of men are immortal I gladly err, nor do I wish this error which gives me pleasure to be wrested from me while I live'. The saints looked forward with unqualified happiness to the eternal bliss in store. A heroic modern martyr like Bonhoeffer saw his execution by the Nazis not as the end 'but as the beginning of life'. But mankind has found a hundred or a thousand different ways of reconciling itself to the inevitable. Speaking as a novice on the threshold of old age, I recognise the need increasingly to prepare one's soul for the finish here and for what comes after. Cicero gives us much admirable advice. 'It is our duty my young friends to resist old age; to compensate for its defects by a watchful care . . . nor indeed are we to give our attentions solely to the body; much greater care is due to the mind and soul; for they too like lamps grow dim with time unless we keep them supplied with oil'.

But no more inspiring message was ever delivered to the old than that of Tennyson in *Ulysses*:

        . . .   and though
    We are not now that strength which in old days
    Moved earth and heaven; that which we are, we are;
    One equal temper of heroic hearts,
    Made weak by time and fate, but strong in will
    To strive, to seek, to find and not to yield.

General Sir James Marshall-Cornwall

KCB (1940), CBE (1919), DSO (1917), MC; joined RA, 1907. Served in Great War, 1914–19 (despatches 5); in Turkey 1920–25; Shanghai 1927; military attaché at Berlin, 1928–32; comdr. RA 51 (Highland) div., 1932–34, maj.-gen. 1934, chief Brit. Mil. Mission to Egyptian army, 1937; lt.-gen. 1938; dep. CIGS (Anti-Aircraft Defence) War Office, 1938–39; dir. gen. air & coast defence War Office, 1939; GOC III Corps 1940, gen. 1941; GOC British Troops in Egypt 1941 (despatches 2); Western Comd, 1941–42; ret: 1943; editor-in-chief of captured German Archives, Foreign Office, 1948–51; pres. Royal Geographical Society, 1954–58; col. comdt. RA, 1939–49; C. Leg. Merit (USA).

'Old Age' is an elastic term, being difficult to standardise since it depends on so many differing personalities. Its length in years is liable to great fluctuations owing to the incidence of wars, plagues, and other aggravating circumstances. Some individuals are obviously 'old' at the age of seventy, while others live to the age of ninety without losing their faculties. In my own case (I shall be ninety-two in May 1979) I do not feel any mental deterioration from the time when I was forty. Physically, I can walk several miles daily on the level, though I get exhausted by climbing hills or stairs. I am slightly deaf, but I never use a hearing-aid, and I only require spectacles for reading small print. I feel quite ashamed of myself when young ladies in a London bus stand up to provide me with a seat.

It seems that people live rather longer nowadays than they did in former times, which is only natural owing to the enormous advance which has been made in medical science and the care of the sick. The Bible is somewhat misleading as regards longevity, for the Book of Genesis assures us that, during the ten generations from Adam to Noah, the average age of these patriarchs was 837 years. Of course the average was raised by Methuselah, the grandfather of Noah, who died at the age of 969; Noah himself lived for 950 years. The next ten generations, from Shem to Abram, failed to achieve this high standard of longevity, for their average life only works out at 367. But Moses, or the clerk who transcribed his first book, may have left out a decimal point, for the Bible tells us elsewhere that the normal expectation of life is seventy, though some are strong enough to live to eighty.

We can certainly exceed these figures nowadays; Lord Hunt (of Everest fame) while climbing in the Caucasus encountered a peasant aged 107. In February 1979 the oldest woman living in England died at the age of 110. Personally, I have no wish to live so long, as I should probably then be a burden to my relatives and a bore to my friends. But I think that I could well carry on for another five or six years, bar accidents. When I was a young subaltern, after a rowdy guest-night in the officers' mess, we used to chant the following ditty:

Old soldiers never die, never die, ne-ver-die.
Young soldiers wish they would, wish they would, wish
– they – would.

In spite of wars, there are many instances of military longevity. General Sir Hubert Gough, who commanded the Fifth Army in 1917–18, was fairly healthy when he died at the age of ninety-two; Field-Marshal Sir Claude Auchinleck, who now resides at the foot of the Atlas Mountains, will be ninety-five on 21 June 1979.

I was fortunate in surviving two World Wars comparatively unscathed, though in the first one I was frequently under fire. During the battle of Neuve Chapelle, 10–12 March 1915, in which the British First Army suffered nearly 13,000 casualties, I spent a morning in the front line of our attack. A German field-gun shrapnel shell burst within five yards of me, leaving seven bullet-holes through my trench-coat, but only grazing my chin, easily treated with a first field-dressing. I suppose that at times I must have felt the fear of death when bullets cracked past me, but I cannot remember ever being really terrified.

I certainly do not fear the idea of death now, and only

hope that it will remove me painlessly before I become senile or chairbound. As regards what happens after death, I have no real convictions. In church on Sundays I repeat, rather mechanically, the words of the creed that I: 'look for the resurrection of the dead and the life in the world to come'. If that will enable me to meet old friends and loved ones, so much the better. Anyway, I can now sit back contentedly and repeat Ovid's pentameter: *Jam veniet tacito curva senecta pede* (And now let bent old age approach on silent foot).

Catherine Marshall

Author of 'A Man called Peter' and many other books. Re-published from 'Something More' (Hodder & Stoughton).

As we grow older the pace and dimension of physical life must wind down. But it is meant to be just the opposite with the spiritual life – growth at an ever-accelerating pace. The heights and depths of the spirit and enthusiasm for God isn't for children. In the latter half of life, the normal Christian almost breaks into a jog or a run. Excitement and aliveness build. A new quality of joy is given to us. It has little to do with the circumstances of our lives – good or bad – but everything to do with knowing Him who is managing the circumstances. It is joy that has the feel of permanence, even of eternity about it. Deep within we know that nothing that befalls us today or tomorrow can ever defeat that joy.

Sir Frederick Mason

*Diplomat. KCVO, CMG. British Ambassador in Chile, 1966–70 and
to the United Nations in Geneva, 1971–73.*

Doctor Johnson said that 'once you retire your perceptions
become sharpened'. Now the great Doctor said many fine
things but that I think was not one of his best. It is all very
well too for Dylan Thomas to tell us that 'old age should
rave and burn at close of day'. The fact is that we get rather
tired, physically and mentally as we grow old. Can we then
rave and burn?

Well, if it means raving against our lot, against the wicked
world, the follies of youth and the madness of politicians –
of course we can, however old. But Thomas didn't mean
that of course. We old people can and do rage as the glory
slips inexorably away. The world seems day by day to hold
more beauty, more complexity, more mystery than we shall
ever be able to grasp. So we content ourselves – when the
rage is stilled – by savouring what does come our way with
all the faculties that remain to us, realising that each hour
becomes more precious than the last.

Then we look back too in wonder and surprise at our own
past life. Now is the time to laugh at our own follies and
mistakes, and to sigh over our lost opportunities. How
strange our earlier selves now seem to us! Could I really have
been such a pompous ass of thirty? Was that love-sick youth
really me? He *was* me then; and although I am another person
now the miracle of memory still binds me to him.

Then come the gentler thoughts of friends past and present,
now dying fast around us. They were after all what mattered

96

most; and in lingering over them in our minds we find that we have after all retained and fostered one great capacity, the capacity for love. Our heart has grown fuller and – surprise surprise – embraces more of our fellow creatures than ever before. They say that the daily grim record of human crimes and bestiality which we absorb through the press and radio must dull our sensitivity to pity. Not, I think, among the old. We may weep at times, but don't think we are necessarily senile.

So we come nearer to Death, and having qualified for the Old Age Pension you begin to look it in the face from time to time when you are not too busy digging the garden or catching up on all those glories mentioned above. Personally I expect at sixty-five to enjoy quite a few more years of active life. But you never know and automatically and often subconsciously I begin to make provision for it in various ways. The family creep increasingly into my thoughts, bringing deep comfort from the knowledge that they will be there after me and remember me until their time has come.

But just as important are the thoughts about values which age sixty-five and thereafter provoke. Now or never is the time to work out your priorities. It is a commonplace to say that; it is also easier said than done. Yet it is remarkable how easy it is to cock a snook at some Matters of Importance (and People of Importance too) at this moment in your life, and how suddenly the little things loom large.

Bertrand Russell's father said he looked forward to death 'as calmly and unmovedly as one who wraps the drapery of his couch about him and lies down to pleasant dreams'. I haven't got to that stage yet; and I prefer to think that when the time comes it will be more than just 'pleasant dreams': by then perhaps these last years will have brought dignity and reconciliation with the mystery awaiting us all as we leave this lovely world of ours. '*Pervixi: neque erim fortuna malignor unquam eripiet nobis quod prior hora dedit*' (I have lived. And even if Fortune turns more unkind it will never take away from me what the Past has given).

Madeleine Masson
Writer

Dear Lord, it is thoughtful of you to send me your Servant,
The Angel of Death to prepare me for the long voyage to your
  Blessed Land,
So far, all I have heard from him is the beating of his great
  wings
Which blot our the dear, familiar noises of birdsong and of
  the
  countryside.
As yet the perfume of Paradise does not block my nostrils
Against the fragrance of woodsmoke, roses and new-mown
  hay.
Dear Lord, when the moment comes for your Servant, the
Angel of Death to lead me to You, give me the strength and
  the
  desire
To leave my earthly home and to forget the shining morning
  face
Of my son, precariously balancing my breakfast tray in his
  great clumsy hands.

The Rt Hon. Lord Maybray-King

Formerly Speaker of the House of Commons. Author, philanthropist.

It is difficult for me to write subjectively about old age. Much of my life has been spent in helping others. Now that I am old, self becomes even less important. One has lived a full life, with its joys and griefs, with its triumphs and failures. If at no other time, the evening of life is the time to think of the young, to help them, if possible, to be spared some of the things our own younger lives knew . . . two World Wars among them.

We have achieved much for our children. My father left school and went to work when he was eleven – his mother worked at the age of seven. Secondary education for all our children, as distinct from the old division which provided elementary education for most of our youngsters and secondary education only for those who could buy it or who were clever enough to win scholarships. The open road to the university. Family allowances. The ending of diptheria – a child-killer until a quarter of a century ago. When I was a boy some children in my villages had rickets – a poverty-disease.

We have abolished poverty – or at least the poverty which existed when I was a boy.

There is so much yet to achieve.

I suppose I am a 'square'. I could never look back on my youth and British society of that time as Justice Shallow did in Shakespeare's day when he both foolishly and falsely exclaimed:

'Jesus the days we have seen!' On which Falstaff commented, 'Lord, Lord, how subject we old men are given to this vice of lying!'

We had very little money. But somehow we seemed to get more value for it than folk do today. I do not mean by this the obvious decline in the value of the pound that has gone on for centuries, though perhaps not so swiftly as today. The things we bought *lasted*, or if they became defective, some craftsman could replace a damaged part, even *make* a new part. Recently an American author has attacked the age for deliberately making goods not to last. He describes how somebody wanted a new door handle for a refrigerator, and was told that the only thing she could do was to buy a new refrigerator.

What we could not afford to buy we made. We made our own happiness – in friendship, in singing round an old organ or piano, and, like Borrow's gipsy, found it in the 'wind on the heath', sunshine, even storms.

But this is beginning to sound a little like old Justice Shallow. For instance, the present spread of 'do it yourself' is indeed a return to the kind of life we led and can be productive of much real happiness in this age of ever-increasing leisure.

It would be easy for an old man to lament the coming of the permissive society. But those of my age know that much of the 'morality' of the earlier years of this century was on the surface only, and that modern freedom and frankness and knowledge would have been a boon to many parents who had children that they could not afford to have, and were prevented from much of the joy they might have had in love-making if they had had the help and advice now so freely available.

Having said that, one still fears that real values are slipping. Home and Church were powerful forces in shaping the *mores* of the old society. Both have weakened.

It ought to be impossible for there to be born today an unwanted child. Yet we still have many a child born out of wedlock (I hate the expression 'illegitimate child', for there can be no such thing truly). And many a child has even now to be taken into care by the authorities because parents have proved unfit to bring them up.

Against this must be set all the boons of the welfare state – family allowances and the protection of the great national health service. There was far more child-misery, malnutrition, disease, neglect, in the days of my youth. And though there were good homes, I lived in a village where the worst families were indescribably worse than the worst ones today.

There were fewer temptations. The peril of drug addiction was hardly known. Today it is a menace that threatens society as never before.

But if there are new sins, the old ones were terrible enough, and we have at least rid ourselves of much of the social injustice under which they thrived. And our youngsters, for the most part are coping with modern times, and are taking fullest advantage of the opportunities which their grandparents rarely knew.

Perhaps one of the most striking features of this day and age is the vast improvement in our care for the old. The first old-age pensions were introduced in my youthful days – much to the annoyance of reactionaries who believed that such pensions would sap the rugged independence of the working-man. Pension-schemes have steadily developed and improved. No old person faces old age with the financial worries that my grandparents feared would come upon them when they were too old to work. There is still much to do in this field – increases in pensions lag behind the rise in the cost of living and in the incomes now received by wage-earners.

I have lived long enough to see the end of the workhouse. As a boy my father told me of a song, 'Let them sleep in one bed', a protest against the separation of old couples when they went to the workhouse.

We are building more and more small purpose-built flats for elderly people, and more and more 'homes' where some twenty or thirty old folk can live, with their own private apartments on the one hand, and communal amenities on the other. 'Meals on Wheels', and 'Darby and Joan' clubs are providing hot meals for thousands of senior citizens.

It has been my privilege to visit a number of special homes provided by voluntary groups – the Methodists for one example, the British Limbless Ex-servicemen for another, and a third a splendid Home for Retired Teachers. In all these we are providing what many need in old age – security and companionship.

Geriatrics is almost a new branch of social medicine, and specialists and nurses are studying and making great advances in the care and treatment of the old.

Again, in this field the demands outstrip the supply. A voluntary body called 'Help the Aged' raised last year a million pounds to provide special housing, extra clothing and amenities for aged people not only in Britain but in less fortunate parts of the world. Of this million pounds £100,000 was raised by young folk – just one example of the way in which our youngsters are shouldering social responsibilities.

In the care of the mentally handicapped, both young and old, we are making advances too. We have learned to distinguish between the kinds of handicap – we now speak of the 'spastics', the 'spina bifida', the 'autistic', to mention only a few of the groups each with its own problems, each with its own specialists on the one hand and groups of parents and friends on the other.

Recently we have made the local education authorities responsible for the education of all children, no matter how abnormal or subnormal they may be.

As for oneself and one's own growing old, I have never seen the sense of lamenting it or of envying the next generation its increased opportunities.

The pessimist who wrote the book of Ecclesiastes, described in magnificent poetry how faculties decline as old age creeps upon us, and urged us to remember our Creator in the days of our youth, before the limbs and sight and hearing grew feeble. This may be wise advice. We that are old know with Omar Khayyam that the past is past and that the moving finger has written, 'and having writ moves on'.

Browning was more optimistic. He wrote:

Grow old along with me!
The best is yet to be,
The last of life, for which the first was made

and:

My times be in Thy hand.
Perfect the cup as planned!
Let age approve of youth, and death complete the same!

The sad feature of old age is the losing of friend after friend. An exquisite old poet, Henry Vaughan, wrote:

They are all gone into the world of light,
And I alone sit ling'ring here;
Their very memory is fair and bright,
And my sad thoughts doth clear.

For the old man has his memories – some sweet and some bitter. Yet with time the bitterness of the sad memories is eased and becomes bitter-sweet, for Nature in this at least is kind.

And nothing can take away the joys we knew, the love and happiness we and our lost friends shared together.

On the other hand, old age brings a new joy – that of grandchildren, and to some even of great-grandchildren. There is a kind of renewal – a vicarious renewal may be – of one's life in the young of one's own flesh and kin. Wider still is the joy of reaching out to help other youngsters, and especially those who are handicapped. To these we must add the joy of helping other folk not so strong, not so fortunate, as one's self.

One old writer said: 'Old men's lives are lengthened shadows; their evening sun falls coldly on the earth, but the shadows all point on the morning'.

Paul Maze (aged 92)

DCM, MM and Bar, Légion d'Honneur, Croix de Guerre. Painter.

... I have to confess that I have not yet reached the stage when I limit the possibility of life – may be I am so taken up by my work and instinctively observe life and humanity. Even in war the problem of death did not affect me – yet I saw much of it. I feel grateful certainly for the providence which has brought me safely to being ninety-two years of age and still looking forward – Death it would seem is not a question of age – I have been and feel privileged to be active and grateful for a long and interesting life – I have of course been conscious of death from early life and accepted its inevitability by the fact of being alive with gratitude!

Yehudi Menuhin

KBE (Hon.). Violinist. Jawaharial Nehru Award for International Understanding, 1970. Decorations include Gold Medal Royal Philharmonic Society, 1962, and many others. Philanthropist.

I would like to say . . . that a happy old age must be the reward of a good life.

I wish people would live more in terms of the riper years and preparing for them, rather than in terms of squandering time, as it were according to the motto – 'we only live once'.

Dr Niel Micklem

Psychiatrist and analyst.

Youth and age, or the ancient Roman sequence of *puer, juvenis, vir* and *senex*, are but two of many ways man has seen fit to divide this homogeneous process we call life into stages. Every division from two to ten has found expression in folktale, literature or the various art forms, but, whatever the sequence, old age is there. This stage of life which nearly all approach reluctantly as if it were a mistake in nature's otherwise acceptable pattern is surely no more possible to avoid than it is to prevent the arrival of winter or the setting of the sun.

Is this true? Can old age really not be avoided? Surely a rational mind will say it is eliminated by dying young. If old age is conditioned exclusively by the flesh and its degeneration as time runs out, then indeed an early death in infancy will avoid it. If on the other hand old age is a stage of life, one of those divisions of a pattern ingrained deeply in every human soul as blossom and fruit are ingrained in every seed, then its avoidance is surely no more possible than that of death itself. *Puer* and *senex* are present in every soul, but we tend neither to recognise nor respect this.

There are indications today that old age not only brings problems, but is itself becoming a problem. A stage of life is losing its meaning and old age is very unpopular. We grasp greedily at longer life, but the prevailing attitude towards it is one of denial, rejection and even elimination, so that the paradoxical situation has arrived in which medical science can prolong life in a way hitherto undreamed of, yet would gladly be rid of the products of its success. It reflects significantly on our culture that the medical services are so closely involved with old age that the new medical speciality, geriatrics, has evolved to 'cure' it. The attitude which has allowed old age to become a problem closely linked with medicine exposes it to the danger of being mistaken for illness. Life's winter, intimately concerned with preparation for death, is threatened with the label of an illness in need of treatment. The word senility, although its roots are in senex, has now largely lost its connections with old age as a stage of life. Today it holds the diagnostic significance it has gained as a servant of medicine and refers to a state of illness which psychopathology joins to psychosis and medicine's physical counterpart sometimes sees as arteriosclerosis or cerebral degeneration. It is a word in frequent use, and as illness it demands cure. The 'very foolish, fond old man' without whom, like the babe in arms, our picture of life would be incomplete, is in danger from society. He stumbles his way repeatedly across our path and is quickly sent for professional help. The danger he may meet is an inappropriate activity thrust upon him and 'treatment' for a state which is not illness. With the best of intentions, that vital inward search as preparation for aloneness and the goal of life is inadvertently prevented.

There are many who understand the significance of this stage of life intellectually, but who, on an instinctive level, fight against it. On the surface is genuine involvement with good intention towards the ageing, but in the depths is denial and an inner attitude which makes mockery of the earnest efforts to help. As human beings we need our neighbour's help, but old age does not need to be treated, cured or, indeed, eliminated in euthanasia. We know nearly nothing of the transformative and creative processes which take place before death, any more than we know – in spite of the fantasies of psychoanalysts – of those in the new-born babe. What we do know is that as the one arises out of a state of unconsciousness at birth so the other is sinking and progressively vanishing within unconsciousness as it approaches death. Both stages show a considerable physical dependence on other people and both share relative submersion in unconscious happenings. These are matters beyond the grasp of our limited awareness, and it is presumptuous to assume they require healing any more than they need to be exterminated.

Death fares little better than its precursor, old age. Earlier times were better equipped than ours to accept death, even to see it within the meaning of life. The present day has a more neurotic adaptation of an unhealthy fear, embarrassment and even denial, a development which coincides with the differentiation of man's rational, intellectual functioning and the astonishing strides made in recent centuries in mastery over matter. There is little left of which we do not know the cause, how it works and therefore how to solve or 'cure' it. Death is part of the residue.

It seems to me that crucial to this picture is our limited appreciation of time which is conceived in the manner most fitting to exclusive rational functioning. Time for modern man is the rate of change as witnessed in matter, the serial time of the chronometer, the moving hand with a past becoming a present and disappearing into a future. It leads to the experience of degeneration, decay and death as an inevitable and meaningless end. This is the chronological sequence of events as the sands run out, with undeniable authenticity in the world of cause and effect, well established and proved by science. It has assumed such importance that the serious possibility of any other mode of appreciating time has almost disappeared. This horizontal movement, prodigious and unavoidable as it strides through history, forbids the time to reflect on another dimension, a vertical intersection cutting time at the present, the ever-present fullness embracing all time and immortality, reaching on the one hand into memory and on the other into expectation, meeting and uniting again in the rounded fullness of the moment. With the implication of a circle it is nearer to the way time was experienced in earlier centuries, and it remains just as significant today as then, though rather more embarrassing to the limitations of a science caught in the grips of space and time as dictated by the chronometer.

Why is this so important? Because to conceive time in its vertical fulness as well as its horizontal dimension is not just an invention of the intellect to correct an unsatisfactory situation. It is an expression of how the human psyche experiences time when not blinded by the light of ego-consciousness. Psyche is not bound in our familiar dimensions of time and space, and there is more to life than a depressing, monotonous sequence of events dictated by the law of cause and effect. Though it is contained in all the great religions of the world this fact lies sadly unheeded. It needs scientists to penetrate the attention of modern prejudice, and there are now those few who begin to see again what was familiar to the wisdom of the ancient world, that there is significance for people in the coincidence of events and their relationship, belonging as they do to all time in the fullness of the moment. Events which seem casually unrelated have until recently been dismissed as unworthy of scientific or serious attention and therefore not quite real. With their dismissal or denial as 'just chance' much of its meaning indirectly vanished from life.

In chronological time are the experiences in which we try to find meaning. In the fullness of the moment is the meaning through which we experience. Recognition of this neglected dimension does not answer the unanswerable question 'what happens to me after my death?' but it does light the way towards a greater significance in life, of which death is the goal and old age the immediate preparation. In the fulness of each present is embraced youth and age, death and life itself.

Naomi Mitchison

Farmer and author. Long experience in politics and local government, mostly in Scotland. Tribal mother to the Bakgatla of Botswana.

Gradually one's friends reach retiring age and one thinks, well, anyway, one will see more of them. But those who have been busy become quickly busier, often at less foreseeable times. There is an immense demand for people who have been good at their jobs to join committees and councils, to do this and that, to help with the vast mass of decisions which have to be made and the amount of work which, since it is not profit-making, has no salary attached, only, sometimes, expenses.

Yet they are the lucky ones. Those who have not made a recognisable, professional life of their own, may be dropped by society; it has no more use for them. They may have spent years and years doing dullish work and at first it is wonderful to have Monday off. And Tuesday. And Wednesday. But then? They may have been admirable wives and mothers, but a generation has moved on. They have to look beyond the home, but if you haven't done this for a life time, it's not easy to start.

In a period when technology is moving very fast and dragging social change alone with it, old people have much less place than in a stable, unadventurous society. For that reason one expects a higher percentage of political conservatism in an elderly group: not that it makes any difference, they can't stop technology any more than one can stop a moving train. In a money-dominated society such as Euro-America, technology is bound to flourish. Every new invention, if cleverly marketed, means profits. And we old ones can't keep up. Quite small children, as we know only too well, have a feeling for machinery, for how things fit together, for what kind of car that is and why the dishwasher – obviously! – is not working. They may not know which fruit in a hedge can be eaten and which not; they won't know the names of quite ordinary flowers. Milk comes from bottles or cartons, peas from packets. The knowledge of centuries is useless to them, at any rate for the moment. Conceivably they may need it some time, but perhaps not. We mustn't insist.

I spend part of my life in Botswana, in a tribal society where the old are still respected, even though technology has got going and, what is more, we have a family-planning clinic. But it is thought – and they may be right – that our accumulated experience can be used as wisdom, even for dealing with the modern world. It is up to them whether they take our advice, but at least we shall be listened to with a certain politeness. When I first went there, it irked me to be referred to as 'the old lady' but now I know it was intended as real respect.

Of course there are fewer old people there; life has more hazards. So those who survive, especially if they are willing to impart their experience, are the more valuable. It is not always possible to be tender in the tough African environment, but the relationship between grandparents and grandchildren is a very tender one.

This makes sense in a society that moves very slowly. Contrast it with America, where the generation gap seems so enormously unbridgeable that middle class elders are urged to go and live as senior citizens in communities specially tailored for their needs. Presumably the elderly poor cannot afford this and must live unwanted with their families, but as so many of them are Puerto Ricans or blacks, it is presumably supposed, by those who guard the American way of life, that this is all right. Maybe it is. If so, one up for black and Puerto Rican manners!

One of our own main difficulties is of course housing.

Most families live in as small a house as they can feel comfortable in; it seldom includes room for grandparents, especially if it is council housing. The sensitive elderly are embarassed and unable to make themselves a place, the insensitive can be a thorough nuisance to the younger members of the family. The best arrangement, perhaps, is living near younger bits of one's family, but not on top of them. One of the snares, of course, is the feeling that so many of us have, that the body is doubtless old, but the mind is ever so young. That may lead to difficulties; it is most unlikely that one is genuinely thinking in the same terms as younger people. It is not a good idea to set out on certain kinds of adventure; bones are more likely to break. One is not quite as good at that foreign language as one thought one was. Above all, one tires.

I am probably very lucky. I have a house big enough to hold quite a lot of people, in a place beautiful enough to make them want to come. All spring and summer they turn up, in quantity during the school holidays. In August, when I have a couple of students to help, we may sit down well over thirty. We eat through sheep, mackerel, fruit and vegetables; I get lots of help from children and grandchildren and indeed almost everyone. And sometimes I am sitting at the head of the table and it is like being inside four glass walls. The contact has slipped. And the sudden exhaustion comes at one.

This onset of remoteness is disconcerting; one has to make an effort to get out of the glass box and be nice to people. My husband and I had plenty of disagreements and irritations, as all married couples are bound to have, but at least we always had contact. Now, without him, the feeling of alone-ness in a cheerful crowd can be dizzying. What will happen next? The answer seems to be obvious. One is no longer in complete control of nerves or muscles; one's balance has gone; the body, which has been one's friend, becomes neutral, an occasional enemy. The time may come when one can only be friends with certain bits of the brain.

That, luckily, goes on. My memory for immediate things which I ought to be remembering has become very bad, as is almost inevitable with age. But if I am writing a book I can keep it all in my head and, if it is a historical novel, for instance, the whole period is clear, not perhaps the boring dates, but the sequences. *Pourvu que ça dure!* Rock-climbing goes, but swimming seems to go on fairly indefinitely; one should keep that up.

At the end one dies, as everyone has done and will do. Surely we are adult enough to accept this? What exactly the total process is – ah, that remains an interesting question, something to look forward to. I remember my father with pneumonia, in an oxygen tent, but looking deeply interested as he took his last few breaths, as though he were noting every moment of an interesting experiment. I only hope to avoid the regression of a terminal illness in hospital, making it impossible for one to keep one's interest going, and I trust that, if I am in the care of doctors or nurses, I shall not be lied to, as, for instance, my brother was by a reputable surgeon, nor yet kept un-necessarily alive after I have ceased to be able to think properly. I hope to avoid great pain since that too is shattering for the mind; it would be nice if some use could be made of one's body. Even quite aged eyes are still useful for transplants. Whether any kind of personal consciousness survives the death of the body is something one doesn't know. There are other and, I think, more interesting possibilities.

However we should try to make things reasonably simple for those who have to clear up afterwards, throwing things away or at the least putting them into order and labelled. But it is surely wrong to try to exert power over events after one's death. It will only make people dislike one. Death, like love, should be taken easy.

Patrick O'Donovan

Journalist. On staff of 'Observer'.

There are many things seriously wrong with death. There is the dreary certainty of it coming. There is the horrid uncertainty over when and where it will come – though that is an uncertainty that can be violently resolved. There is the additional uncertainty over what, if anything, lies on the other side and few men of religion can believe in the after life with quite the same certainty they bring to the rising of the sun or the eventual arrival of the 27 'bus.

There are the pain and humiliation that go with it. There is the end of the experience of life and, I suspect, very often a sad and lonely disappointment that you did not use this experience better. Death is essentially unknown and threatening and what men do not know they fear and what they fear they hate. Only the more hysterical patriots and saints court and long for death.

A long acquaintanceship with the death of others appears to make no difference. Death *can* come almost graciously and arrive as an act of mercy, though one would have preferred that such an act of mercy had never been necessary in the first place. It is said that executioners, doctors and priests die hard. It seems to come easiest to those more ignorant of it, to the young who die in battle with almost everything of experience to lose. There is also some cheating and unidentified God of Battles who allows them to believe that it will not happen to them. For life, when you are young seems infinitely long. Or at least it used to seem so.

This fear of death is, I fear, a condition of life. The sixteenth-century poets cry '*Timor mortis conturbat me*', is still as real and human as a longing for a drink or a cup of tea and far more urgent. It is possible a little, especially in company, to assuage this fear by a designed levity. After all death is only another bodily function and all of them, from eating downwards, are basically ridiculous and ugly. This is an ancient and unfashionable heresy but empirically true.

I have tried to make light of it all. I have had the staircase enlarged so that my coffin can come down decently. Countless generations of men have minded about such preposterous details and have taken them seriously. And then I have a decent little collection of grave sites.

There is a place in a Catholic graveyard in a Catholic village in Lancashire which I am told I can have. I am entitled to a plot in our Anglican cemetery here which would be nice since children play there and it seems to get a lot of sun.

Then there is a wild cross-roads graveyard in that part of Ireland from which my grandfather came. I am told I have the right to be buried there, though the place, raised up now high above the windy fields, looks dangerously overcrowded.

And there is another. I was, some time ago, having tea with some nuns in the same part of Ireland. Somehow it came out that they had plots to sell and I took one for ten shillings. The Reverend Mother said it had a lovely view over the sea. It did. She also told my wife it was solid rock and would cost £200 to get down to the proper six foot. But I still have the receipt and have claim on a bit of useless Irish granite. Or perhaps the Reverend Mother sells it to all her visitors.

But levity is not of great help in the face of the looming facts. When, after the Black Death, Europe had lived with death as if it were the master of the house, they seemed to embrace the horrors that could not be postponed. Grief for the death of children was numbed and art, sophisticated and simple, went on and on about death like a drunk trying to make little of his affliction by talking about it.

There is no cure for this fear. But men and society try to face it. A great state funeral is an almost triumphal assertion of the dignity of man in the face of this indignity. And no one thinks what now lies within the box, or, if they do, they do it alone and shudder away from it.

It is a triumphal assertion that we are as little furry animals that lie like squashed gloves on country roads. The lordly words of the funeral ceremony may clash with your memory of the way in which your friend died, and yet they make sense – partly because they were unconsciously written for the living.

But if you can swallow or even nibble on the premises on which those words and chants are based, it does become less necessary to evaluate this thing in clinical and humanitarian terms. The fear will remain and the pain may last too long. But the process of dissolution at last makes sense in terms that, alas, can never be quite fitted into the finite language of humanity. But then I cannot be quite certain. I have not experienced it yet. And when I do – and I certainly shall – I shall be too preoccupied to come back and report.

Marchesa Iris Origo

DBE, FRSL. Biographer and essayist. Holds honorary degree of Smith College and Wheaton College, Mass. Member of American Academy of Arts and Sciences. Isabella d'Este medal, Mantua, Italy. Republished from the introduction to a section of her anthology. 'The Vagabond Path' (Chatto and Windus, London, 1972).

Confucius used to say that it was not until sixty that 'his ears obeyed him', and therefore, according to Po-Chü-I, the years after sixty were called in China 'the time of obedient ears'. Certainly the later years of life are the time when men may acquire a greater delicacy as well as firmness of taste, and sometimes also a greater capacity to pay attention – not only to works of art, but to their fellow-creatures and the universe. This attention is due not only to experience, but to a greater detachment: one's own self is no longer so much in the way. 'God knocks at every door,' wrote Julian Green, 'but who ever opens? The place is taken. By whom? By ourselves'.

Simone Weil called this kind of attention 'creative attention' and believed that no real understanding of other human beings is possible without it. 'Creative attention', she wrote, 'consists in truly paying attention to what is not there. Humanity is not there in an anonymous lifeless body by the side of the road, but the Samaritan who stops to look is yet paying attention to that humanity, and his subsequent actions show that his attention was real . . . In that moment of attention faith is present as well as love'.

Yet another prerogative of old age may be – though not always, since mind, senses and heart may also be dulled by illness, or by that daily companion, fatigue – an increase of a different sort of awareness. Proust referred to it, when speaking of memories of his childhood, as a return to his upper consciousness of certain events, certain emotions, which in reality had never stopped. 'Of life', he wrote, 'I have been increasingly able to catch, if I listen attentively, the sounds of the sobs which broke out only when I found myself alone with Mama. Actually, their echo has never ceased; it is only because life is now growing more and more quiet round about me that I hear them afresh, like those convent bells which are so effectively drowned during the day by the noises of the streets that one would suppose them to have been stopped for ever, until they sound again through the silent evening air . . . '

The 'beauty of the physical world', too, may in old age recover some of the clear intensity that it had for us in childhood. What we shall, perhaps, not often see again becomes as marvellous as when it first met our sight. And sometimes, also, the human scene takes on a fresh pathos. 'Happiness' – I am quoting again from Simone Weil – 'is an object for compassion for the same reason as misfortune, because it is earthly – that is to say, incomplete and fleeting . . . Compassion for fragility is always bound to a love for true beauty, for we feel intensely that things which are truly beautiful should be granted an eternal existence, and they are not'.

Reflections such as these give a fresh perspective to a man's knowledge that his days are numbered, and may lead some people, according to their turn of mind, to 'tune the instrument here at the door'.

For the practising Christian there are other hopes, deeper certainties. Yet these, too, falter, and I have personally found it consoling to read that even Père Teilhard de Chardin, 'le grand imaginatif', wrote a few days before his death: 'The difficulty of old age is to fit one's interior life to a life without a *future* for oneself. (One has one's face to the wall)'. He added, however, soon after, " 'To be ready' has never seemed to me to signify anything else than to be 'stretching forward' ".

There are some 'last sayings' which I have thought of quoting . . . since they used to please me . . . But on re-reading, there are

119

only a few that I now find credible – at least with the high-flown significance generally attributed to them. Goethe's '*Mehr Licht*', for instance, may surely have had no deeper meaning than that his sight was failing, and there is something too pat about Heine's famous phrase: '*Dieu me pardonnera: c'est son métier*'. To Beethoven's saying to two old friends, '*Plaudite amici, comoedia finita est*' (Applaud my friends, the comedy is over) – I prefer the simpler remark on his last day, when two bottles of wine were placed beside his bed: 'A pity, a pity, too late'. I also like Madame de Pompadour's remark to the priest about to leave her bedside: '*Un moment, Monsieur le curé, nous partirons ensemble!*'

A touch of irony, too, is often more moving than edifying phrases. I like Lady Violet Bonham-Carter's reply when her daughter bent over her and asked how she felt: 'Amphibious'. And, especially, I enjoy the comment of the Englishman who, surrounded by a circle of anxious friends, opened one eye and said: 'A watched pot never boils'.

Ruth Pitter

Poet. *Hawthornden Prize, 1937; E. Heinemann Foundation Award, 1954; Queen's Medal for Poetry, 1955; Companion of Literature, 1974.*

It is as natural to grow old and die as it is to be born and grow up; and yet we feel it is so lamentable to be on the way out, especially if we are ailing, or lonely, or frightened, or comfortless. But there is no getting round it; everything that is born must die; indeed, one can die without even being born. We used to think of the life of the unborn as an ideal state, but now we know better. The unborn have their troubles. They can certainly be ill; it is thought they can be unhappy. The ordeal of birth looms over them as the prospect of death looms over us. Birth itself must be a great shock for the infant. The suffering of the mother is so obvious; that of the infant tends to be overlooked. Mercifully we forget this trauma at the very outset of life, and so it does not occur to us to sympathise with the baby as well as with the mother. But the rage and grief expressed in the noises young infants make, the thought of their helpless dependence, and of the unknown terrors that these new humans may have to encounter, make me just as ready to say 'Poor old baby!' As I am able to say 'Poor old soul!' at the sight of a miserable old man or woman.

The baby is not blamed for crying, and I feel that old people should not be blamed for grumbling, which is much the same thing. Pain and discomfort, sadness and deprivation, demand an outlet. 'O that my grief were thoroughly weighed!' cries the Psalmist: and this is a perpetual human cry. 'O that my case were honestly considered!' 'Listen to my tale of woe!' And this perhaps points to the necessity of listening patiently to the old one's long recital of symptoms and wrongs; of unfeeling relatives, disagreeable neighbours, shrinking purchasing power, bad health, bad weather, bad news, unsympathetic medical staff, and disobliging feet. Old wrongs, old griefs, old aches and pains, old everything; and the one great positive reassuring fact, that we shall soon be done with it all, quite overlooked.

[Perhaps *I* could get a grumble in at this point. I don't see why I should write this article, in pure goodness of heart, and not get a rake-off for my own emotions. I have most of the regulation grievances of the old, but I have in addition a few that are perhaps not so widely shared, or not so widely realised: and mind you, the *unrealised*, undefined sense of wrong is just as depressing as the wrong we *can* focus and express; very likely more so. Here goes then. *I want quality back.* I want real bread and cheese, real beef and mutton, real beer, real linen, woollen, and silk. I want numerous and competent tailors and dressmakers, because I hate reach-me-downs which never quite fit. I want real leather boots and shoes made to measure at a reasonable price, so that I may walk and not be weary because of the very uncharitable character of modern footgear. I want knitting wool that is worth knitting up; this is more important than many realise. I want - to name but one commodity out of the lost legions I mourn for – I want the good dried fruit back. Fellow-babies of the Boer War, do you remember the Christmas dried fruit, mountains of it in the grocers' windows? The plump Valencia raisins, meaty muscatels in their own clusters, 'bold' Vostizza currants, big soft prunes, apricots, peaches, and pears? There would be a few stones among the sultanas, but to pick these out from among the beautiful fruit was a child's diversion . . . I want the clean, comfortable, civil railways back; promises kept, not broken; children taught to be kind and honest as a prime necessity. And I should like to feel once more (only I never shall) that if I can save sixpence, it will still be intact, 'like a hand-wrought nail driven into an oak post', twenty years later.

That was a nice refreshing grumble. And I could have gone on a lot longer; but perhaps I am a disagreeable old creature, and must not try my readers too hardly. In fact, I do feel a little guilty.] I wonder if we grow old as nicely now as people used to. I wonder if we have rather fallen into the way of expecting life to be quite all right, and as though it wasn't fair that we should have to put up with anything we don't like.

I wonder. In 1930, my mother bought a cottage in a little country hamlet; and as it happened, she had several neighbours of ninety and over. When I think of them, I am ashamed. Now, anyone who was ninety in 1930 had been brought up in the 1840s – the Hungry Forties, when it was hard indeed for a poor man to provide for his family. These veterans remembered the bad times well: but not with resentment. Rather in an old-soldier spirit; triumph in having got through, and warm satisfaction at having an unlooked-for pension – a pension which, for the women at least, was often more than they had earned in their prime, small as it was. And they regarded life's ills as an integral part of life, and bore them no grudge.

I have not the slightest doubt that the strength of these people was derived from their Christian upbringing, which of course hardly anyone, at that time, would have dreamed of questioning. The Ten Commandments and the Sermon on the Mount had been their sheet-anchors. Of course life was full of troubles; but they looked to One who in his short life had trouble enough, 'from his poor manger to his bitter cross'. Courage, kindness, and gratitude were the rule among them rather than the exception. They would often raise their eyes and hands to heaven in thankfulness for any little gift. I am glad to have seen this. It is often mentioned in old books, but I suppose it has quite died out now. It was very pretty; it reminded one of the action of a small bird which elevates its beak after drinking – to make the drop run down of course; only people used to say they looked up in gratitude. (But I remember one old dear who declined a gift. It was a bunch of grapes. She explained apologetically that grapes were more for gentry, and would disagree with her).

[Out of a throng of memories I choose one, of a very poor old widow. She lived with a bad-tempered daughter; there wasn't much peace in that house. Here she comes, the gentle aged creature, sure of her welcome: 'Kin I set by your fire a bit? I 'ont be no trouble, and if you've nothing partickler for dinner, I 'ont stay'. (Good manners; she means that if a proper meal is being cooked, she will be glad of a share; should there be only left-overs, she quite understands that a guest might be one too many). 'The spring come on fast now. Don't forget to save me a bloom when that lovely rose come out; I'm so fond of that . . . So Topwell's gel got married the other day. It put me in mind of my own wedding; that were on the very same day, more than sixty years agoo. The min (men) washed the best waggin, and kivered it with evergreens and stuff; and we set in the waggin on cheers (chairs), and the min drew it to church. Oh, I hed such a pretty gown and bonnet, all over rosebuds! And my master give us a whole leg of mutton for our dinner. And we was very happy.

'But I lost my first little gel. She'd hed the measles real bad, and she didn't get over 'em, but pined away; not quite four year old. And a day of two before she died, she say to me, 'Mother, I'm a-goin' a long way – kin I wear your pretty wedding bonnet?' Oh, that were a trouble! I were carrying my second daughter then – the one I live with now; and I reckon it was the trouble I was in that made her so quick-tempered, poor thing! I niver cast it up to her; you see it ain't her fault; it was the trouble I was in when I was a-carrying her, my poor gel! So I goo and set in people's houses when she's a bit put out, to take myself out of the way . . . Goodness me, that's niver a bit of roast veal you've got there? I don't know when I last hed a bit of roast veal! Mrs. English give me a slice of roast pork the other day, and roast pork is real nice; but a j'int of veal is a treat, if you like! . . . Oh dear, I always say that a day in your house is my little bit of Heaven!']

There were those two who had lived together, in the cottage that was now falling to pieces round them – I remember opening a cupboard door and finding myself in the garden – for at least seventy years. The husband, as a young labourer, no doubt very much in love, had saved four pounds (goodness knows how) to get married on; but his father fell ill, and the young man acted *like* a man, putting his ardour into second place, and spending his four pounds on doctoring and medicine. But he was very sorrowful. He thought, 'If I only had the price of the ring, I'd marry and take my chance!' Then one inclement winter morning he was ploughing, and he thought he saw something gleam in the fresh furrow. He stopped his team – now what in the world could show so bright after being buried in the dark soil? Gold; it could only be gold, which nothing can tarnish. He picked the small object up, and rubbed it; and it was a ring, an ancient gold ring with a 'posy', as they used to call inscriptions on rings; and this one said, 'Keep faith; till death'. And with this Elizabethan ring the pair were married.

They were poor, of course. The old wife would explain: 'We had to allow his mother sixpence a week for an extra loaf; she had only the parish half-crown; we couldn't see her starve'. Perhaps it was only their being childless that enabled them to afford the sixpence. But in the end, in their extreme old age, they could no longer look after themselves. They had to be taken into the infirmary; and the sad thing was, that there they had to be separated, into the men's and women's wards. This was desolating to them. However, the old lady would soon have a birthday, and her husband was to be allowed to come to tea with her.

The birthday came, and passed; but the husband did not come to tea with his wife: he was dead. The old lady was not told that day; they hoped she had forgotten. But as she was being settled for the night, she said to the nurse, 'Oh, wasn't it lovely to see Tom again! And how well he was looking! I can see he's being well looked after; I shan't worry about him no more'. Keep faith, till death; and after?

And after. Do you know, now I'm old, I think so much about the resurrection of the body. It is such a curious belief, strange beyond words! and yet it is at the very centre of our Christian faith; indispensable, *crucial*. The simplicity of our forebears on this subject has faded; it was bound to do so. When we look at Stanley Spencer's great joyous spring 'Resurrection' in the Tate Gallery, with all the dead in the village churchyard popping up among the hyacinths and daffodils (all in their Sunday best, too) we smile affectionately, as one smiles at a dear old folk-tale. And yet, surely, we may still smile affectionately: wherever love goes, we may go; and we know that love has indeed passed that way. Whatever its ultimate meaning, the resurrection is there for us, if we claim our share, and bear our share, in the sacrifice that procures it. And yet, though we have been assured that the resurrection is something so glorious that no one in the flesh can possibly imagine it, we go on wondering 'How?'

It must at least mean that everything will be all right, in every way, and for ever: that it is so now, if we could only perceive it. What? all the grisly deeds of the past, all the possible horrors to come? All the sufferings of the innocent – man tormenting man and beast, beast tormenting and preying on beast, the whole pile of age-old suffering and wrong? Yes, surely. I am not sure that theology would approve, but this is my own idea. We tend to think that everything that has happened is for ever. Fixed in time; fixed in the past; fixed in history. Nothing can alter it; the blood of Abel cries out for ever. But take a closer look. What is Time? Eternity is not Time; Eternity is itself. Do you think that after all Time is so real? Are you not a little suspicious of it – might it not be merely a mode of our perception, our *fallen* perception? Do you believe that nothing can alter the past; that God himself cannot alter it? I Believe he can; I believe he does; I

126

believe that for those who aspire to eternity, the atonement has power to *unhappen* the past. Time, of all things, may be the most unreal. The very event in time is to be wiped out, if we accept the sacrifice made to that end; and we can pass clean into the new creation. 'Time is, time was; but time shall be no more!'

[Many modern ideas tend to be destructive of faith; but there are some extremely modern ideas which to me are quite the reverse. It's true that their originators might think that I make very improper use of their material; but somehow I think that Sir Bernard Lovell, at least, would not be unsympathetic. To me, as far as I can understand it, modern cosmology has distinct possibilities in regard to the resurrection of the body; quite different from anything science could have offered us even so recently as thirty years ago, when we thought our galaxy (our little galaxy, only one of countless swarms!) was all the universe there could be. The more we know, the greater becomes the mystery, and the greater the possibilities. '*Nothing* is capable of ultimate explanation!' '*Omnia exeunt in mysterium*'.

But if still we cannot help asking 'How?' we may perhaps think of those awful states of matter that scientists are beginning to postulate in the enormously distant 'pulsars' and 'quasars'; matter under such stress of its own nature that all the physical 'laws' we know, and think so immutable, are transgressed, denied, swept aside; and then comes the mighty, tentative suggestion, the strangest and most pregnant hint, that these objects may ultimately be expelled from our universe, and pass into another; not into another region of this creation, but into another universe, another creation altogether: where, who knows? they may be regenerated; for nothing in *this* universe can regenerate them once they have collapsed. 'In My Father's house are many mansions'].

I would be content to go out, to cease utterly, when I die. There is nothing to lose by that. But if I accept Christ, I accept his terms. If he accepts me, I become a part of the divine Life itself. To that I trust, as a swimmer may trust when he dives through the great oncoming wave, and breathes again in the sheltered trough behind it. On this planet I have seen some of the infinite wonders of God. This earth, with its air, its water, great range of elements, stupendous variety of life-forms, is so different from the sun's other planets, so very different, that they – poor frozen or torrid, lifeless, monotonous, dark of distant bodies – might almost be mere mechanism, mere counter-weights and balances, to keep this rich and beautiful earth in orbit, triumphantly waltzing round its own star, and bearing its glorious and terrible burden of humanity. Surely I have had my share, and would gladly accept mere cessation. But I have no choice. I am commanded not to be beguiled by time, but to know that I am summoned to be a part of the whole everlasting glory.

'Thou, Thou art Being and Breath,
And What Thou art may never be destroyed.'

'What, mother? Have they left you all alone?' 'They left me with my God'.

Brigadier Lord Porritt

GCMG, GCVD, CBE. Formerly Governor General of New Zealand; Sergeant Surgeon to HM the Queen; President Royal College of Surgeons (1960–63), Royal Society of Medicine (1966–67), British Medical Association (1960–61); Member of International Olympic Committee and Vice-President (lately Chairman) British Commonwealth General Federation. Surgeon, soldier, statesman, athlete, author.

To grow older is a natural biological progression; to grow old – at any rate for an intelligent person – is a pathological admission of failure to adjust to one's environment. The former – 'senescence' – is totally inevitable; the latter – 'senility' – is largely preventable!

These may seem hard words, but the organs and tissues of the human body do, in the ordinary course of events, wear out, some more rapidly than others. The process can be hastened or delayed according to various factors in life – genetic inheritance, economic and nutritional conditions beyond the control of the individual and social and occupational environment. Such factors form the basis of the so-called 'chronic diseases' – many of which incidentally occur in younger age groups – and also of the fair wear and tear which is 'growing older'.

Physically the changes of old age are irreversible – no panacea has yet been found to deal with them – neither by the magicians, herbalists and quacks of medieval days nor by the high-powered scientists, research workers and medical men of the twentieth century. It is a very true statement of fact that from the moment we are born we begin to die – but the process, especially with today's living conditions is often lengthy – and for the vast majority of people is physically, only relatively if at all, uncomfortable. One should surely consider one's self fortunate to grow older; it is a privilege denied to many in this rapidly moving age in which we live!

The 'normal' infirmities of old age – slower locomotion, some degree of loss of sight or hearing, can in today's world, thanks to modern developments in medicine and science, be to a very considerable extent dealt with or at least considerably ameliorated.

But what is the individual's personal responsibility is the mental, intellectual, and if need be, spiritual aspects of growing older. And this applies equally, if in varying degree, to the white-collar worker or the no-collar worker – and perhaps even more so to the man who does no work at all. Only by accepting such responsibility can he avoid the wastefulness, the sadness, the loneliness of growing old.

And such things should not be – they are preventable. Old age is but one stage of life – and in the course of nature it should be both enjoyable and constructive. After all have we by then not added to such knowledge as we possess, the great benefit of experience – and for the fortunate, the conjunction of those two assets – knowledge and experience, leads to the inestimable gift of wisdom.

And yet how often do we not meet an old man of forty years of age – with so much of life already unappreciated simply because he has not the will or the courage or the sense to get outside himself and realise his enormous potential. Equally, of course, to be impartial one has to admit to meeting and knowing young men – perhaps too young – of seventy or more! But who would doubt that the latter's fate is to be envied the more!

To grow older, but not old, demands – except for the favoured few who are born and live with a continuing extrovert personality – a conscious and positive mental effort which, however, in the course of time, becomes reflex. This effort requires the cultivation of initiative, the nursing of enthusiasms, the preservation and development of every possible interest and hobby. Of course all this to a degree must be limited by physical factors – but it is amazing how much can be achieved by the free and unfettered use of those

130

three essential senses – the sense of values, common sense and (perhaps essentially) a sense of humour.

Probably the most potent force in developing this type of life-preserving temperament is a continuing concern for and interest in people. The richness of life lies very largely in one's reactions to friends and to acquaintances – and in fact to strangers, who after all are only friends one does not know. And this is a wealth that does not diminish with age. Contemporaries may get fewer – but young people and children provide a compensatory challenge and joy.

Old people and younger generations have a very special relationship – they can understand and appreciate each other even with wide difference of values and objectives. The fresh stimulus and enthusiasm of youth reacts naturally to the maturity and experience of age. There is a mutual respect – and trust.

Old age should never be looked upon as a time of fading dreams and melancholy sadness. Old people are still alive – and life goes on apace around them. Always within the limits of physical disability – often minor and surprisingly often negligible – it should be lived with enjoyment. Despite all its troubles and difficulties it is a very wonderful world in which we live and age should allow one to savour and appreciate it all the more for having known what it was.

An extrovert's view – yes, but a pipe-dream – no! It is quite possible to live a life, as against just existing, to an advanced age if one only uses the gifts God gave us – and puts a little bit of effort over the years into augmenting their practical uses! The older one gets the more should the mind dominate – and be able to dominate – the body. The inevitable stage of life which we have called 'growing older' then becomes a time of mature thought and fulfilled wishes, of challenging ideas and high ideals and of deep enjoyment and warm friendships.

But even the best of things ultimately come to an end and every one of us must sooner or later face up to that end – death. I am talking of the final episode of the natural wear and tear process – death from old age – not violent or accidental death. It is unfortunate that the very word 'death' should hold such sinister overtones. It is surely much better thought of – and pondered upon when the time approaches, as cessation of living. I have always remembered the last words of one of the 'Lusitania's' victims – 'Why fear death? It is the most beautiful adventure of living!' This gives it the right slant – a unique experience, which, despite all the years, one has not previously been able to indulge. Men fear death exactly as children fear the dark – from lack of knowledge of the unknown. But the unknown is adventure and should therefore in thought be looked upon as challenge – to one's faith, to one's courage and to one's intelligence.

For the comfort of those who still harbour doubts, let me say as a doctor, that only on the rarest occasions does a person apparently know they are actually dying; nature seems to have developed some wonderful mechanism that translates the last weeks or days or hours into a semi-conscious, sleep-like state that can only be described as restful peace. Do you remember Spenser's *Faerie Queene*? 'Sleep after toil, port after stormy seas, ease after war, death after life does greatly please'.

If the failing subconscious at this testing time does in fact experience 'pleasure' – a possibility that frequently observed outward and visible signs makes rational – then surely fear should not be allowed to enter into the concept of death. And death (from old age) is not painful; it is in fact very often a release from intolerable discomfort.

Of course it would seem that one's belief is likely to be the dominant factor in the mosaic of one's last hazy thoughts. Faiths are multiple and universal, but beliefs are one's own – individual and personal. And it is they that have grown up and been nurtured over the years – belief in the beauties of nature, belief in the essential values, belief in people, belief in oneself and belief in an omnipotent Being.

Given these, it matters little whether one envisages a future life or is content to think that one lives on in those with whom one has come in contact and to however small or great a degree produced some effect. Either way the comfort is there, either way the thought must cushion any sadness in passing on to the great adventure of death.

Live an old age happily and to the full – and then it would seem likely that the cessation of life will be complementary and equally happy and peaceful.

Kathleen Raine

Poet and scholar. Republished from 'Faces of Day and Night'
(Enitharmon Press, London, 1972).

1. *Death - as known by the Body*

Erotic love, we are so often told – so much too often because
it is only partly true – is a self love. And so, no less, is grief
over the death of a friend often self-grief.

It can scarcely fail to be so. For at our first close encounter
with the idea of death the very cells of our bodies seem to
change.

Almost on the first occasion I ever came close to a death
I envied the dead playmate for whom this great terror was
past, while for me it was still to come. How such a very
ordinary, not even very clever or brave or religious child had
known how to die – the most difficult thing in the world to
imagine let alone to do – I could not conceive. For I myself
could not endure even the thought of it. It was my body that
cried out against death. My blood seemed to flow backwards
in my veins, my limbs to be paralysed. I could scarcely draw
my breath, and all possibility of joy seemed gone from the
world. And my sorrow was all for myself.

Death was nearer than I had supposed. I had always believed that my life was charmed. And so, I had supposed,
were the lives of all those near to me. And now, a child that
last summer had played with me had died. And in an instant
my flesh and blood and bones had told me what they had
always known, though I had not – that they had been dying
all the time, that I belonged to death from the moment I was

born. I had thought that they were all the time growing and extending their life into the world like a plant. Now they opened to me the other secret of the cells: 'We are dying', they told me, 'from the moment you began to live. And the death that you have begun to die is your life. Your life is adying'.

It was in May, and the earth was green and growing. My father, to distract my mind, took me, I remember, for a walk through the sunny lanes. But the bright sunlight was to me as black as an eclipse. I tried to reach out towards the growing plants. But they too seemed to spill their corruption everywhere. I remember that I picked a little purple flower with soft leaves, and smelled its freshness. Then my memory gave me its name, that came lile a shock of pain into the wrist of the hand that held the plant even before I knew why. Deadnettle. The very vegetation was rank with death. The tall pollened grasses in the hay-meadows seemed as remote from me in their growing and ascending life, as the most distant stars. Nor could I by any means touch the green hem of the earth's garment. If I could only reach it, I felt, life would flow into me again. But I could not. The green fields were black, the flowers black, and every shadow in the lane was the symbolic pall of mourning hanging over the dead. My father, as I walked beside him, was calm, as he was always calm, his gentle Christian face open and kindly. So I clung to his hand. His hand alone, as I walked beside him through the May greenness, held me on earth. If I let his hand go, I would slip over the precipice of nature, fall out of the earth, my home, away and away into a desolation of non-existence. My father's hand held me like an anchor.

When for a moment I felt my father's mind straying away from me, I feared that even his hand would not have the power to hold me on the earth. How brave, I thought, of my father to walk alone, serenely, when death was present everywhere, in the grass, in the air, in the animals, in himself. While the whole living world was dying, there was my father walking calmly in the sun, enjoying the fields and the wind-

135

ing lane, and the view of the distant hills. Did he know what I knew? Or had he some secret knowledge unknown to me? Did he accept calmly the body's provisional life? Or believe in the soul's immortality? Or did he live so constantly in the Kingdom of Heaven that his own life and death were no longer of great importance to him? Whatever it was, that Christian secret strength alone upheld me on that terrible May walk in the fields, when all the trees except the Tree of Heaven withered and turned to dust.

But at that time I did not know my father's secret. Nothing, as I had experienced it, could exceed the knowledge that my body had of its mortality. For the body is so absolute. It knows without doubt, with utter certainty. And it knows only what it knows, and forgets all that it has known, and does not guess what it may know. Its power of carrying conviction is so great, and yet it remains a poor person; and its ultimate fate is to become its terrible opposite, a dead thing.

Clearly there could be no disproof. The only possibility of escape from one state of knowledge is into another. One can know so many things, exist in so many states, the one knowledge for the time excluding any others. The body can know that it is alive no less certainly that that it is dying. But at this time, so completely did my knowledge of death fill me, that I could receive no other.

My old kind aunts, and all people other than myself, seemed to live in a living world, I in a dying world. They could not reach me, nor I them. Indeed, when they spoke I had to think what their words could mean, for they referred to objects that were, for me, no longer what they had seemed in a world that scarcely existed, a mere tenuous film over the darkness of annihiliation. They seemed to be speaking to me from a long way off. And the distance was impassable, for it was in myself that it lay.

I recovered in time, and the ghost of the world, the spectral surface below which I had seen death's features, became dense and solid again and the sun came out – as when a real eclipse passes. I still knew what I knew, but the knowledge no longer filled me to overflowing. It grew smaller, like a healing wound, and became only a little core in me. And yet sometimes on a clear and happy day, death would stretch itself out in me again, and fill me with denial of life and remind me that though for a time I had forgotten it, my body was always at every moment dying. At such times I dared not sleep lest death take me unawares. Or if my finger bled, the wound seemed to go in and in to my mortality.

That was long ago, at the edge of childhood. At the peak of its life and growth the living and growing part of me refused to accept the passing and dying. Now the impulse to live is less strong, and death has made some progress in my flesh and nerves and bones. I have come to be at home with sleep and insensibility, so dreadful to all feeling youth. Some day perhaps the body will even welcome its death. Even now it has long ceased to take a tragic view of its mortal nature. Nor does the earth, now, seem less lovely because it is transient and insubstantial than if it and I myself were as solid and durable as I once so innocently believed.

2. *Death – as known by the soul*

Once I was so far advanced into death, that I was for a time without the world at all, without any foothold for my senses on the thin texture that upholds human life. Or so it seems to me as I remember or imagine an event that perhaps never took place. Though indeed there is nothing so rare about death that a human being may not claim some acquaintance with it. At the time, however, I gave no such name to the happening that I underwent.

I do not speak of illness – I was not ill for long, or painfully – indeed, I remember very little about that. I speak of a conscious, painless, but quite distinct impression that remains of an excursion outside my body.

I remember the iron-cold winter, and walking on a drinking trough in a field covered with thin ice. It was a silly thing to do, not so much because the ice was thin, as because it was a pointless and not very enjoyable game. The ice broke, and I was plunged in cold water to the waist, to the dismay of the more cautious and sensible farmers' children with whom I was playing. I was eight and a half years old at the time – the oldest child there on that occasion – and I therefore determined to brazen it out. I pretended that I was not at all wet, and that I did not mind, and knowing that I had done wrong I was afraid to return to my aunt with wet boots and stockings, and skirt and coat. I would stay out till my clothes were dry, I thought.

After that, I remember hours of miserable cold and shivering, and at last I returned home. But even after I had been undressed, I could not stop shivering, and my teeth chattered. It was not painful, and I laughed at it; my aunt laughed, too, to console me, and put me to bed, not in my own bedroom, but in the best spare bedroom, in a great double bed, with a feather bed on it, that was to keep me warm. It was probably very damp. Anyone who has lived in an old house in the north country through the winter, knows that those stone houses that stand strongly against the wind, cannot keep out the cold and damp of a northern winter, that rises from the ground and creeps through the walls.

As I lay ill, I became oppressed by an extreme obsession with the visible objects in the room. It is not only the spectral world that can haunt the tenants of the visible; but the visible world itself can loom up before the mind with the force of a phantom that will not be shaken off the tormented senses.

I first became aware of the blue wallpaper in the room, with a white lozenge-shaped design in diagonal stripes. The lozenges began to group themselves and to confront me with faces, that stood for what nature of being I knew not. I scrutinised them and wondered, and tried, by re-arranging the shapes mentally, to bind these Klee-like apparitions. There were patches of damp where the paper was crusted with a white salt-like lime. I lay and made mental alterations of the lozenges and the patches of damp, and became anxious because the apparition of the lozenges could not be held in the order of any pattern I could discover.

A text embroidered in cross-stitch on tapestry by my aunt when she was young, troubled me too. 'I am the true vine', it read; and a bunch of grapes and a bright green leaf endorsed the words. Knowing as little of the vine as I knew of God, I did not understand the meaning of this arbitrary assertion of my aunt's cross-stitch, the colours wrong in places, telling me 'I am the true vine'; equating two unknowns in an assemblage of red and purple and green crosses. In this, too, I felt the immanence, as with the lozenge-faces on the wallpaper, of a riddling protagonist, whose game consisted in piercing together the objects before my eyes in order to convince me that things were as these phantoms would have them, and not as my reason or wishes told me they should be.

The truth, of course, was just the other way. This mirthless enchantment that seemed imposed on me by the material objects about me was the trick of my diseased senses that turned these innocent creatures into tormentors.

Over the fireplace, a large illuminated page with scrolls and gilded lettering and blue angels blowing uplifted golden trumpets, puffing out their tiny cheeks, read, 'Children, obey your parents in the Lord, for this is right', – then followed the Fifth Commandment in Victorian script, faded too with damp. I tried to anchor my delirious mind to the beauty of the angels. I tried to read beauty into their gowned and floating forms. But one was too fat, and aroused in me only dislike, and the other angel, though I loved it as much as I could, failed me at last, and beauty flickered out of it, like a mirage in a desert. These sensory deceptions troubled me as I tossed and turned in my hot feather bed. My joints ached, and I was too cold and too hot, but above all, restless and anxious because the patterns haunted me, and the angels flickered out and would not save me. And then the haunting stage passed gradually into the loosening of those ties by which the senses bind us to the sensible world. Instead of bearing down upon me, the world began, slowly, certainly, to recede.

It was solemn and wonderful, the unloosening of the ties that held my body. Partly it was like drunkenness, the whirling of the walls of the room round me, accompanied by a sort of low humming in my ears like water. Partly it was like being led by one of the angels – for one is never quite alone. There is always some companion, a table or a flower or a house or an angel. At first my body seemed to have no bounds, and a sense of vastness and weight filled me. That was pleasant, for it required no effort to slip away into that vastness. But quite suddenly I was no longer allowed to be passive and to slip away. As if a dancer were to remove his mask to reveal himself as the thing in itself that he has, until now, only represented; as if the symbol were to change into the reality itself, the event became fraught with awe. There was no dancer, no person present save myself. But the solid room, the solid house, began to grow thin and spectral, and to cease to give me support, to hold me in the arms of the world. They were no longer solid, and the unknown, the dark, mastered the tiny power of the known – the familiar room, the embroidered vine, the illuminated angels, the lozenges on the wallpaper, the rectangle of light with six panes that was the window. But my eyes were closed, and the sky into which I went was another sky, with no sun. The world grew small, until it was no larger than a toy castle under my foot; and I left it, though some fine clue still tied me to it. I found myself remote in a strange space, neither dark nor light, neither day nor night. It seemed to me that with me was a being with two swift wings, but featureless; and with this small-winged angel, if such it was – my own angel – I was leaving the world with its insubstantial walls, and taking flight to another star. It was very solemn, very strange, but at first I went without question, without fear. I believed that I had a destination, though I never reached it.

For I do not know why, I wanted to return, I became afraid. I did not want to leave the earth, I remembered it, I remembered life, and the house, and the room with pictures on the walls, and the crops and the moors; and I struggled against the flight with the winged seagull of my death. All was confusion, like a troubled pool, until I returned to that little room in a north-country manse, with trees and sky outside the window, and my mother giving me water to drink from a silver teaspoon. She seemed glad to see me. And I too was glad, now, to be in the human, banal, imperfect world, to see my mother, and my aunt, and all the very ordinary, safe, and imperfect things near me. Nor did I think at the time that anything very strange had happened. Children die so easily, or so easily recover. To me it was very easy to come back. And I told no one.

I was not nearer God, nor farther, when I left the crumbling illusion of the world with the small, two-winged angel. Only it was a different existence. It did not seem strange, for some such experience we must all have once, when we die – and perhaps more than once. I may have imagined these things. But I think it is like that to die. The illusion of the world crumbles, one remains in space that no longer affords a solid foothold. The world is insubstantial to the spirit – is that so strange? – and we are entirely and only ourselves.

But whatever the nature of the cause, I have never quite forgotten how then the earth and sky were rolled up and packed away and forgotten. I was glad, on that occasion, to return. For a picture seen is brighter than one remembered. And since then, I have seen many beautiful fields and trees and flowers and streams and birds. I have leaned over bridges in London, and looked at the muddy Thames; in Cambridge, and loved the slow weedy Cam; in Stockholm, and watched the round nets swirling in the Mäler; in Paris, where the plane-trees stand in the dust by the Seine; in Brittany over old bridges with daisies growing in their crannies; in Westmorland, over my own bridge, where the dipper buitt and spleenwort clung. And the waters of life have flowed past me and through me. I have wept and laughed; been in the arms of the man I love; walked in the fields with my children on summer evenings. And even to-day, I see sky and trees and earth and my table covered with letters and books, these pinks in a hyacinth-glass; the portrait of a soldier drawn in pencil by a friend; and the little earthenware ash-trays made for me by my children at school.

For these things I returned; for the scent of the jasmin flowers I am wearing; the warmth of the gas-fire on my ankles; the sound of 'buses in the King's Road. Was it worth it? Who am I to say? Worth what and to whom? Our work and days are not only, or entirely, or primarily, our own.

But how, once having known the texture of the world's illusion to be so thin, can I have cared so much? Wept for sorrow and for joy, loved and sinned and suffered? How one forgets, how we are made to be deceived by this deception! We are made for our house and our house for us. And it is, after all, no deception. It is rather, one kind of relationship with reality. Why deception? It is true, in its time and place. When we are no longer in this frame, we may wonder why we cared so much for transitory creatures, and did not cleave rather to the eternal things that are with us too. We may wonder. But, again, we may understand better this incarnation, and what it means, this substance of material that we work in.

Dr Peter Riley

General Practitioner.

'Thirty – forty – fifty then comes the nipping frost, some period of agony, that robs the fibres of the body of their succulence, and the hale and hearty man is counted among the old'. I think we would take issue with Trollope to-day over what age constitutes the commencement of old age. I shall take as my definition the years from sixty onwards.

Old age is a physiological process that happens to most of us. Following the period of childhood we pass through youth when growth and development predominate and when intellectual capacity begins, to maturity and adult life and finally to the period when degeneration predominates.

It is inevitable that with ageing the body processes degenerate, that the functions of the body become less dependable, and that we become subject to more ills. It becomes increasingly difficult to see in the dark, the hearing becomes less acute, there is an increasing liability to falls as the joint becomes arthritic, and the thought processes become slower, there is less flexibility in outlook, a resistance to change and an unwillingness to deal with new situations.

The great fear of living too long is that the brain will degenerate so much that one loses one's independence and becomes totally dependent on other people. One becomes a mindless life with little control over bodily functions and so rooted mentally in the past that the present seems too ephermeral to consider.

This breakdown of personality through age is almost a

143

reversal to childhood, existence at a very basic level; fortunately it happens to very few of us and none of us I think would wish to live long enough to reach this condition of life.

Senescence must be seen as a normal biological phenomenon and the fear of old age must be resisted. In primitive societies the number of people reaching old age is limited by the poverty and harsh conditions of life, but the culture tends to regard the old as elders and they are respected and have a status in their society. In modern western civilisations with a high standard of living, a decreasing birthrate and adequate medical care, we have a higher proportion of elderly than ever before, and this can produce strains on society particularly in the sociological field, though I think there are signs in our society to-day that the young are very concerned with the care of the old, as is shown by many young people doing voluntary work in geriatric care.

I work in a rural practice of four doctors with eight thousand patients to care for, and we have about 18% of patients over the age of sixty-five, either living alone or with relatives. We are fortunate in that we have two full time district-nurse health visitors attached to the practice, and we know all the old people under our care. Those who for some reason are housebound are visited regularly by either their doctor or the health visitor, and this ensures that any problem concerning their health or well being can be dealt with.

We also have a purpose built block of council flats for the elderly in the charge of a warden where old people living alone can at any time of the day or night contact the warden should they need help of any kind. The idea of building special accommodation for the elderly is a fairly recent innovation by the local authorities, and in my experience it is a very happy way of keeping people independent for as long as possible.

Those who live in the community, particularly those living alone, can avail themselves of all the social service facilities such as home helps, Meals on Wheels etc., and also the

144

services of a very active Community Care association run by volunteers who organise outings for the old people, and who call to see them regularly in their own homes.

This is the ideal that should be achieved, but there is the opposite situation, the lonely old person living alone, having lost their marriage partner, often rejected by their family, and who, through some emotional or psychological block, refuse any help that is offered.

They are often not capable of looking after themselves, and can live in conditions which in middle age they would not have tolerated. They neglect themselves in personal hygiene and nourishment, and often sadly they have to be admitted to a geriatric unit of a hospital. These are the people who have found it difficult to adjust to the challenge of old age and eventually find themselves incapable of coping with the problems of daily living.

The most important aspect of ageing is, I am sure, to keep the mind as active and free of preconceived ideas as possible. To accept that one cannot perform some of the bodily functions that were possible, and not to try and fight old age by artificial means such as hormone therapy, etc.; this cannot achieve its object because psychologically the desire to regain lost youth can only produce unhappiness.

It is most important to be able to see the point of view of young people, however different it might be from one's own moral and social values, to contribute to the community in which one lives, and to be interested in other people rather than oneself, by this means old age can be rewarding and need have no fears.

Old age inevitably leads to the event of death. It has been said many times that the most important occurrence which happens to us is being born and dying. We cannot control our birth but we can prepare for dying.

As a doctor I come into close contact with death and often in the elderly it can be a release. The very old are usually quite ready to take this journey, they realise that they are very limited in what they can do, they are often very tired

145

and death seems a natural function and something not to fear. The only regret is leaving behind those people one cares for, but here the sorrow is for those who are left.

It is the illness and pain that are often associated with death that surrounds the whole subject with fear. The doctor's work is to ease the passage of death by preventing unnecessary suffering due to pain and by supporting the individual through the final months and weeks of life. This journey is inevitably a lonely one and it is important that the doctor and the relatives must be attuned to each other in order that the dying person has complete confidence in those around him. This is so much easier at home rather than in hospital, and so much better for the patient to be surrounded by familiar things, and where the pattern of life continues as usual.

Pain is destructive of personality and must be controlled, and the fear of addiction to pain-relieving drugs in a terminal illness should never be considered. The important object of care is to maintain the quality of life as near to normal as possible so that the patient may die with dignity and at peace. If the pain is so severe that it cannot be controlled at home, the patient may have to be admitted to hospital, and ideally it should be to a special unit such as the Hospital at Sydenham under Doctor Cicely Saunders, where the standard of medical care for the dying could not be bettered.

It is often difficult as a doctor to know whether or not to tell the patient that he or she is dying, but in fact the situation usually resolves itself easily because the patient if he does not want to know never asks a direct question. However, it is very important that the relatives be told in order that the total care of the patient can be planned. I think that the person who does not ask whether he has a terminal illness can more easily cope with death on these terms. It is a defence mechanism by which he tries to protect himself and his family, and by not discussing the possibility of an end to life he can more easily go through this journey.

However, I personally feel that this situation shows a lack of communication and if two people have lived together

146

through a married life sharing the joys and sorrows of those years, then their relationship should be strong enough to accept the fact that one of them is going to die before the other, and that when the time comes they should help each other through this period in the full knowledge of what is happening to one of them. If this can be achieved the future of the partner that is left can be discussed, the next stage in his or her life or that of the children of the partnership, can be talked about so that with death comes a peace of mind that life will continue in a pattern which has involved both partners.

Many people with a terminal illness will face this prospect with courage, wanting to know all through the stages of an illness what is happening to them. This acceptance of death can be a very rewarding process both for the patient and for those caring for him, and together the anguish can be lessened.

The doctor must give time and he must be concerned. The daily or weekly visit over a long illness is most important and it is during this time that confidence can be built up that the doctor will not fail in easing the way. He must be receptive to thoughts and words, and if there is frustration, depression or anger he must be prepared to rationalise these feelings and to treat them. He must be receptive; the care of the dying is a process of mutual trust, letting the patient be the judge of what or what not to say, and never destroying hope.

What is death – is it just the end of human life, the consciousness of having learned or unlearned through a lifetime of experience – ending in nothing, or is it something greater? – this depends on our philosophy of life.

The meaning of God is love, and it is through love that we experience the meaning of life and why we are here. It is my belief that we enter this life to learn about love and that we go through a series of incarnations until this is achieved. It is through our awareness of nature and of other people, and our response to them that we learn this, and if we are sensitive to the beauty of nature and the suffering of others, and try to forget ourselves, we can achieve tranquillity of mind and death becomes a very natural function not to be feared.

I have had the privilege on many occasions to witness the peace of mind that a philosophy of life can give – the knowledge that death is not far away and yet still contributing to life and giving an example to others. One person I particularly remember, a woman of thirty-four with three children, who was dying of cancer with multiple secondary deposits. We had discussed her dying and she had come to terms with it, and had told her children that she would be leaving them. Although she should have been in a lot of pain, somehow her acceptance of death lessened this as she was completely relaxed and happy. During the last few days of her life she had what I think was a glimpse of the future, and she described it as crossing a river to a beautiful country beyond – she died peacefully in the knowledge of a life well lived.

'If there is no life hereafter then this life is of supreme importance to us. If there is a life after death then this life is of even greater importance'.

Vera Bloodgood Scribner

(Mrs Charles Scribner, Sr). Sculptor (New Jersey, USA).

I have had a very fascinating life, have been almost everywhere in the world, and have known all kinds of interesting
people, most of whom I found, if they really amounted to
something, were free from conceit. Unfortunately I feel that
the predominant emotion of our time is hate, whereas if it
were love in any form it would truly change the world. So
many people appear to be searching for freedom, but so often
in the wrong way, and find Communism.

I love life with all its ups and downs, and as I approach the
end, as now I do, I want to hold on to every minute that is
left. Death I do not give much thought to: why worry when
there is no certain answer. However, I think there might be
something in reincarnation; but, if not, then just a long sleep,
without awakening.

But to return finally to the living: I believe the key to
remaining 'young at heart', whatever one's age, is to share
in the new ideas and interests and problems of young people,
to stay in touch with those who follow a couple of steps, or
generations behind.

John Sparrow

Warden of All Souls College, Oxford. Barrister, author.

Chill on the brow and in the breast
   The frost of years is spread –
Soon we shall take our endless rest
   With the unfeeling dead.

Insensibly, ere we depart,
   We grow more cold, more kind:
Age makes a winter in the heart,
   An autumn in the mind.

———————— . ————————

How long does it take to die?
   A life-time, if you do it properly.

Robert Speaight

CBE, FRSL. Actor and author. Officer Legion of Honour. Fellow of the Royal Society of Literature.

The ceremony of death was familiar to me from my earliest years. The tombstones that lined the flagged path leading to the church porch; the erased inscriptions; the occasional bunches of flowers; the earth heaped up beside the newly dug grave; the passing hearse and the shining brass fittings of the coffin inside – these were all, so to speak, part of the day's observations to the innocent eye. I knew what happened when people died, and what other people did to them; and as time passed the knowledge came nearer home. Death was a prime constituent of the literature that was read aloud to me, or that I read to myself. I remember the funeral of King Edward VII for which my father designed the decoration for the processional route; the end of Scott in the Antarctic; the chorus of 'Nearer, my God, to Thee' as the Titanic went down; and the young officers billeted on us in the early days of the Great War, some of whom were killed at the Dardanelles. Nothing of this was surprising, or even particularly shocking – although it was naturally sad – to a boy who was brought up to follow, for a long three hours on Good Friday, the slow agony of the Crucifixion.

I very soon became acquainted with the sight, as well as the fact, of death; my grandmother in her last sleep, the baby of some poor neighbours who had been carried off by diptheria. These struck me with awe, but not with terror. I remember meeting Mrs Armstrong when she was already jaundiced with arsenical poisoning, and I followed her

151

husband's trial with morbid fascination. A certain morbidity, no doubt, coloured my enjoyment of Edgar Allan Poe. I knew what happened to people who took life long before I had the faintest notion of how life was given to them. My brothers and I were each photographed, I recall, standing beside a tombstone in the churchyard. This was a quasi-histrionic attitude, for tombstones were quite in the nature of things if one had been taken to see *Hamlet* as soon as one could read or write.

Nevertheless the Gravedigger's 'Get thee to Yaughan; fetch me a stoup of liquor' did more than demonstrate Shakespeare's genius for proper names; it sounded life's perennial protest against the outrage of its interruption. At no time have I been even 'half in love with easeful death'. Neither illness nor hazard brought me close to it, and I have rarely gone to bed without longing for tomorrow morning. Tomorrow morning still seems to me the most exciting thing in the world. Nevertheless as one approaches the limits of the Psalmist's span, the day after tomorrow, at least, begins to wear a different aspect. There are so many ways of facing it. W. B. Yeats, when he was closer to it than I am, declared that only two things were still of interest to him – 'Sex and the dead'. I confess that I am repelled by this belated curiosity. If death is the transcendence of sex, so much the better for death; and there seems to me a certain impiety in attempting to prise open the gates which will disclose their secrets soon enough. I do not question the manifestations of the occult when they are thoroughly attested. I only wonder whether, on occasion, they are not capable of a practical joke.

A friend of mine, and a close contemporary – a man who flees morbidity like the plague – has declared that after the age of fifty death is the only subject that deserves to preoccupy the mind. I prefer Yeats's previous exhortation to the soul to 'sing and louder sing for every tatter in its mortal dress'. Yet I can well understand how a moment may come when the song may die upon the lips. If I did not believe that life was a gift, however unwanted, which only the giver has the right to take away, I should be tempted, in those circumstances, to exchange it for what A. E. W. Mason, in the romantic idiom of his time and character, described as 'the hell of an adventure'.

There are few Christian people, I suppose, for whom belief in personal immortality is quite unquestioning. We cannot imagine the hereafter; and that is the limitation of mortality. I should be insincere if I said that I found it easy to believe in the survival of personality after death – whatever proofs may be brought forward in its support. I should prefer to say that personality seems to me so independent of physical decline that I find it difficult to believe in its extinction. If you hold to the doctrine of original sin, however you may try to explain it; if you believe that human nature is flawed, and set in the context of a flawed creation; and if you still believe that God is writing the story, albeit, as the Portuguese proverb has it, 'with crooked lines' – then death may well appear as the punishment for a primal fault in which we all share, and immortality as a mode of compensation for what seems to us unjust in the 'whips and scorns of time'.

It was my sad privilege, many years ago, to assist closely at the death of my younger brother. He was only twenty-six with a brilliant career in front of him. When I wrote of this in a book of memoirs, I said that 'his death had a curiously bracing effect upon all of us'. An unkindly reviewer took exception to this statement; yet it should not have been so difficult to understand. Naturally, we mourned the loss, and the cutting short of the 'bough that should have grown full straight'. But we were also fortified by an example of courage and piety and humour; and braced – there is no other word for it – by the sudden opening of a new perspective upon life itself. By the operation of a mysterious paradox, death had enlarged the dimensions and enriched the content of what it was taking away. If we understood the truth of the old Spanish proverb: 'In life we are in the midst of death', it seemed none the less true that 'in death we are in the midst of life'.

Death is, quite simply, a matter of fact; and although it may remain a matter of regret – even of deep regret – emotion is gradually drained from our contemplation of it. A man dies, and we put on the panoply of mourning. The bell tolls, the drums are muffled, and the guns fire a last salute. But soon his life becomes an episode, significant or obscure, in the human story. He exists between two dates, neither of more consequence than the other. He may be important as a fact of history; his works may live after him; but the anniversaries of his birth and death – if they are remembered at all – are remembered without tears. Whatever we do in life contains an element of choice. Shall I buy this house, or that? Shall I marry X, or shall I not? Shall I follow my conscience or my inclination? But I have no choice as to whether I shall die, and that is why I look forward to my own death as a matter of fact, to be met without enthusiasm, certainly, but also, as far as possible, without fear. Nor can I choose the moment or the manner of my death. I can only choose the frame of mind in which I shall hope to meet it. With resignation and without complacency; with a decency of regret for what might have been so much better, but with face set firm against despair; above all with the consciousness that

> . . . on whatever sphere of being
> The mind of a man may be intent
> At the time of death – that is the one action
> (And the time of death is every moment)
> Which shall fructify in the lives of others.

So – at the last, and never more acutely than at the last – with a sense of responsibility. By contrast, the Epicurean's 'Let us eat, drink, and be merry, for tomorrow we die' is merely an evasion, and the Stoic can only endure with fortitude what he cannot avoid and cannot understand. The Christian can die as gaily as the one and as bravely as the other; but he can also die more intelligently. What invests his passing with significance and dignity is the awareness of responsibility to his Creator, to his neighbour, and to himself. For the revelation which he has freely accepted has taught him what death is about. 'The readiness is all'.

Dame Freya Stark

DBE. Writer and traveller. Triennial Burton Memorial Medal from Royal Asiatic Society, and other medals. Republished from 'Perseus in the Wind' (John Murray, London, 1948).

Teetotallers, as they grow old, must look back with sadness at the shores of their life strewn with refusals – dull little wrecks, split on no reef of circumstance, but tossed and abandoned as it were in weeds. The real teetotaller cannot limit only alcohol. Most things, if he comes to think about them, are harmful in excess: food, and the more transitory ways of love; and Tolstoy added music. Some men might put clothes, some women golf and fishing.

> While Adam in his garden spent
> His hours in a calm content
> His lady engineered his fall:
> She *was* so tired of it all.

It is a sobering, or inebriating, thought that a purist teetotal wife might conceivably prohibit gardening. Gambling, racing, betting, are doomed – and the Stock Exchange too. And one cannot logically prohibit drugs and read the Sunday press. There is no end to it. A Father of the Church had said that 'even of sitting, as of all carnal pleasures, there cometh satiety'.

But a sound instinct in human beings will not respect virtues that are compelled. One of the few advantages of riches is that they make austerities voluntary; and teetotallism strikes directly at this freedom. It strikes at the very keystone of liberty, the principle of freewill itself. It interposes its puny rigid No between man and the elasticity of choice, allowed by the Gods for all occasions. And what principle underlies this impertinence? A mere squalor that holds moderation impossible, and places safety in impotence alone.

Are we able to divorce? We will be unfaithful in love. Are we strong? We will certainly go to war. We sip our glass? We shall overdrink to drunkenness. And now, with governments planning right and left, our ability even to walk about the world and to earn our living and direct our labour is being doubted and fenced in more and more: so that it looks as if we were soon to be teetotal all over.

If this is so, there will be few happy old men left as the years pass, for the contentment of age depends upon a not too abstemious youth. Minds are kept active with enjoyment and there is no reason not to like one thing because one likes another, when there is room for so many. This is why much is forgiven to polygamists and amateurs: while even the special monogamist is only a man who discovers the intrinsic variety of the one. As we follow animals from molluscs or earthworms to man, we see, emerging slowly,

A speck, a mist, a shape –

the figure of Boredom. It is noticeable in dogs, cats and horses, and I am convinced that wild animals die of it in captivity. In human beings it is perhaps the goad to civilisation, pricking the slow team to jog along: and if men, as they say, invent so many more things than women, this is probably merely due to the fact that they often sit about in the house with nothing particular to do.

Moderation must never be pursued like art for art's sake only; but should be pressed out of the fullness of life as a drop that has to unite many savours, so that only a little of each can be afforded in our spoon of time. There are factories for vermouth on the plain of Piedmont, whose mountain scent is wafted across country as one drives. There, beside the sheds and high chimneys, strips are laid out and planted

157

with gentian and thyme, and grey-leaved wormwood that gives vermouth its name, and many other aromatic herbs brought down from the pastoral high valleys: so that when a glass is offered, it holds in a few mouthfuls the whole taste, sweet and bitter, of the hills. Such is life, and the art of it is to judge the mixture of the flavours, so that your vermouth, far from being reprehensible, may do what it is intended to do, and give you *an appetite for more.*

Old age, after well-filled days, learns to distil these substances and test their permanent values, and enters a timeless world where years need scarcely count. There it can avoid such aversion as meets old people who cling to inconstant things, even in slight matter – even in amusement, or in dress. For the shams that youth may wear lose their illusion: lace, silks and jewels must acquire a durable beauty to be tolerable; and any extreme of temporary fashion comes to jar. In personal relations, change must be held no longer clasped and rebellious in its brief prison of the will, but left to ebb and flow, while its unchanging background counts more and more. Failure to attend to these things is, I think, the whole reason for the misunderstanding, so very common in England, between age and youth. Old men retired find the centre of their being in committees still: and women cling to their haunts with haggard looks, like climbers on an ice slope whose feet have slipped, who drag, on the sliding brightness, at those to whom their weight is tied: Youth looks upon them as enemies, since they encounter his ways. 'Besides, sir, there must always be a struggle between a father and son, while one aims at power and the other at independence' (*James Boswell, Life of Samuel Johnson*). I have often fancied how, if I were a man burdened with a career, I should like to be made a consul or vice-consul in a small and unimportant place of my own choosing, with a guarantee that no promotion need ever come my way; so that I might grow into it and love it at leisure, and forget to look at the advancement of others, nor feel their eyes upon my own. There, I believe, knowing one divorced from any thought of power, young men and women would come gladly for advice, safe in the knowledge that the *doing* still rested in their hands. But the fact is that we are a people teetotal about thinking, whatever we may be about drink: and the idea of leisure in obscurity, with *thought* for enjoyment, makes no very general appeal.

It comes more easily in other lands.

I happened one evening long ago to reach Banias, where the river Jordan rises under the shrine of Pan. The Crusader castle of Montfort lies extended upon the height above, and foothills crowd around it and rise with the whole sweep of northern Palestine towards the majesty of Herman. I was visiting this castle but had been caught by the late afternoon; so I enquired my way and spent the night in the house of the Sheikh of Banias, in a room with nine uncurtained windows and a bed of hard bolsters and yellow satin quilts. The Sheikh had never received a European before, nor did he ask even my name, but with their general courtesy prepared the best he had and entertained me, and sent me with a guide next morning: and when I returned, took me up steps to where his mother lived on the top storey of the house, in two rooms with a terrace filled with pots and flowers.

This beautiful old lady was dressed in white, and her face was framed in the white coif of the Druses, to whom she belonged. When we had talked a while, she put her hand on my arm and took me to a balcony. It hung over space where the land fell away from what had once been the city wall. The Jordan danced below, invisible beneath a fluttering carpet made by the tops of poplar trees, through which the gay voice of the stream came singing. The white and green leaves played like shot silk in the wind. And beyond their restless delight the marshland of Hule stretched with black cattle grazing, and wattle huts, and reeds. Beyond it again were the highlands of Safed.

'I have been here thirty years', the old lady said. I asked her if she ever left Banias, or even the house she lived in.

'Never', she said.

'Do you find time heavy on your hands?'

'No', she said. 'When my eyes are tired, I open the window and watch the sea-wind moving in the trees. And when my heart is tired, I sit alone and think of God'.

The West can find small solace in quite such quietude, and there is justification, after all, for gaiety in age. For the joy of youth is the setting out on the voyage, but the happiness of age has achievement behind it and a landfall in sight; it is no small thing to come without shipwreck within hail of one's anchorage: and if one is able still to take pleasure in things that pleased at the starting, in strength and agility of body or elegance of dress, or rapier-play of talk – why, it is so much added, a last sweet-meat thrown to tilt the measure of life in our favour a little beyond the weight we could expect; it is an innocent delight that few will grudge us, if we carry it on the circumference and not in the centre of our mind.

On the whole, age comes most gently to those who have some doorway into an abstract world, – art, or philosophy, or learning – regions where the years are scarcely noticed and young and old can meet in a pale truthful light. We move there with increasing freedom as time rubs out the illusions of possession, whose dark attendant, envy, fades away. The loss of our own things, or such we thought so, our faculties, our friends, our loves – makes us again receptive as in child-hood, though now it is no human hand that gives. In our increasing poverty, the universal riches grow more apparent, the careless showering of gifts regardless of return; our private grasp lessens, and leaves us heirs to infinite loves in a common world where every joy is a part of one's personal joy, with a loosening hold returning towards acceptance, we prepare in the anteroom for a darkness where even this last personal flicker fades, and what happens will be in the Giver's hand alone.

The shared universe, the escape from their own individual cell, gives to the eyes of some old men and women a clear and happy look, a delight for all who follow them to see. It is perhaps more frequent among labouring people, or in

160

countries where the old are accustomed to live with their children and children's children, as is general all about the Mediterranean. This greater happiness does not, I think, come from a greater measure of youth preserved by living with the young: for who does not know the dim old Latin ladies who live among their grandchildren and nieces, with an outline long since blurred in black, and faded from its original contour, negations as it were personified? This very loss of outline makes them happy; it is a liberation from the regards of others, a merging into the current of other lives, a finding of that self which Youth with its hedge of beauty and maturity with its eyes on the target have made unreal for years. By these they were shut away from their right estate, which is nothing less than all the world of men: and the light in the eyes of old age is that of an opening door. One sees it too in old countrymen and sailors, who also merge and forget themselves in a universal world.

I have had the good fortune to know and love a number of such old people, and dearest perhaps of all was my god-father, W. P. Ker. He joined us every year in the Alps to climb, and would say that, if released blindfold on a mountain top, he could open his eyes and know whether he stood north or south of the Italian border: the Swiss and Italian valleys are cut in different shapes. He carried Dante or Pindar in his pocket, and walked with the slow mountain step that scarcely knows a difference in age or youth . . .

On his last climb, when he was seventy . . . we set out for a spur of Monte Rosa through meadows underneath the later stars. When the dawn hit the snows with red spears we reached a high scooped corrie, still cold and unawakened from the night, where the grasses end beside a fanlike stream. Here we drank and rested, and watched the gaiety of day spilling from its high cup; and on the mountain-side an hour or so above, on strong slabs so steep that I had to cut him a resting-place with my ice-axe, he suddenly gave a small cry and died . . .

. . . The place was high and steep. Only space surrounded

it, and rocks and snows beyond. Soon white mists came browsing like cold flocks and hid the habitable world. We sat waiting there for seven hours, watching the changes of death. His face, so dear, lost all mortal lines of age; every hour as it passed brought a new shield of peace. It was not youth that returned, but a beauty neither of life nor time, and yet himself, as we had divined him but never seen beneath the little waves of living. The features, so familiar, and majestic now, seemed in their estranged borderland of mortality to be one with the mountains about us, in that place where the oldest laws of earth and the most enduring are listened to alone. Men came from the village and laid him, wrapped in a blanket, on a ladder, and carried him down across the snow; and we followed him with pacified quiet hearts, as if we had seen no sudden interruption, but one who in his progress reached a porch and stayed a while with the inner majesty of the temple already upon him, before he went on his way.

The Rt Hon. Sir John Stephenson

Lord Justice of Appeal.

I like old age. I think that I always have. When I was a small boy, I liked to imagine myself an old man. I would walk with a limp. I had a great-uncle who was not only old, but a bishop and a bishop with a stiff leg. I greatly admired the swing of that gaitered stiff leg and swung one of my gaitered legs as stiffly as I could in self-satisfied imitation of 'Uncle Bishop'. I even wished my hands would shake like the hands of old people, and copied their trembling when I thought no one was looking. I suppose I must have regarded it as wrong for the very young to pretend to be very old; or it may have been fear of ridicule which restrained me from playing the old man when grown-ups' eyes were on me.

I am not sure why I liked the idea of being old when I was young. As I grew up, the advantages of old age became more obvious. They were the advantages of being grown-up, being able to do what you liked and not what other people told you to do, with something added which was not easy to define: dignity, wisdom, the respect of others, an established position of your own, a life lived at your own pace and to your own orders. And as I grew up, I, like my father before me, found the society of the old congenial, more congenial than the society of my contemporaries. The older people were the nicer they were to me – or so it seemed to a shortsighted, unathletic, priggish little boy and youth. I dare say the middle-aged seemed old to me then, but I liked people to be really old. The generation gap I liked was a gap of two generations, or even three.

How pleasant and how easy (I thought) to be a grandfather! Closer relationships were and would be strained by difficulties of every kind. It was hard to be a good son, impossible to be a good brother. As for the roles of lover and husband, how could one hope to choose wisely or to play them well? I had the misfortune to be born without grandfathers; but I had two splendid grandmothers and I was rich not merely in uncles and aunts but in great-uncles and great-aunts.
(I could even boast a great-great-aunt, a vainglorious boast because she was younger than my grandmother). In anticipation I would readily reverse my relationship with the older of them and adjust myself comfortably to the part of a well-loved grandfather. What my accomplishments might fail to bring me simple length of days would supply; I dreamed of the year 2,000 when after seeing the 21st century in I should celebrate my ninetieth birthday surrounded by admiring descendants.

In my daydreams I gave myself another three years – why I stopped short of my century I do not know, but so it always was. It was not until later that I became acquainted with that marvellous old man drawn by Dürer in 1521 and by him recorded as in possession of all his faculties at that very age. I wonder how much longer he possessed them and at what age he died. When I first saw him in facsimile in Dürer's house at Nüremberg, I thought again how good it would be to jump the intervening years and go straight to being an old man.

But there was no short cut to old age. To death, yes, but not to old age. The blind Fury with the abhorred shears might slit the thin spun life at any time and old age never come. However there was no counting on an early call and there was much to do and suffer before reaching the haven of old age.

I have reached it. With a shock I find that I have passed the entrance without noticing it and am writing about old age from the inside. I shall be sixty-three by the time these words are published (if ever they are) and even today, when so many inhabitants of our life-preserving civilisation are older, a man in his sixties – with a grandchild – must recognise that he is old. My mother went on regarding, and even revering, others as old when herself into her eighties; and I expect to do the same; but whenever youth slipped into middle age it was many years ago; and however late in life middle age shades into old age it is not as late as this.

But if this is old age it feels very different at sixty from what it looked like at six or sixteen. Dignity – where is it? Wisdom – where shall she be found? Some establishment of position perhaps and some slowing down of tempo certainly, but life goes slower chiefly because you can't keep up, not so much because you don't want to. Yet there is a pleasing fulfilment of expectation in that you are free to order your life in your own way. Not as free to be unsubtly selfish as the Victorian paterfamilias, but free to do more what you want and less what other people think you ought to want. Not only are orders much fewer and opportunities for disobedience blessedly reduced; the tyranny of convention has lost its grip and the effort to be like others at their most ordinary, which bedevils the life of the schoolboy and even stifles the individuality of the man, is mercifully kept within rational limits, if not bravely – or lazily – abandoned altogether.

Yet even at the beginning of old age come warnings that with greater freedom further restraints are on the way. The body begins to play you false. Things that it has done for you without calling attention to itself it now can do no more without effort or hurt. You move fast and are breathless; you turn suddenly and are in pain. Aches and pains come easier and take longer to go; cuts take their time to heal. Eyes, even myopic eyes, focus with more difficulty; ears, even good ears, may not seem deaf but require others to speak more distinctly than before. The mind too starts to play tricks. Memory, tenacious of the distant past, becomes strangely

165

selective in what it now retains. As for proper names, will they come when you do call for them? The answer to Hotspur's question is an emphatic No. The only names that come readily come wrong, and to find even the most familiar may be the subject of painful and often unsuccessful research. Add to these limitations, which cannot be hid from the old man himself, many another which attracts the attention of his family, his friends and neighbours and those who see him at work, if he is lucky enough to be still at work: the closing mind hardening with his arteries into sluggishness of purpose and insensitivity to new ideas. If the leg does not stiffen, the mind will: even if the hands are steady, the resolution wavers.

I doubt if the natural man can welcome these changes, for they are, and he must recognise them to be, signs directing him downhill to his approaching end – to death, call it by what euphemism you will. Only great misery of mind or body will make a man hurry down that hill before the very last few paces, or take his own leave of life before starting or completing the descent. I remember helping to defend on a charge of murder a man who had gone off with a girl to die because they could not face life without each other and could not live together. They both took a heavy overdose of sleeping pills, he cut her wrists and his own, and after three days and nights in the open he astonishingly recovered and found her dead by his side. In those days the survivor of a suicide pact was guilty of murder and murder was capital. He therefore wanted to plead guilty to her murder and to join her as he had intended. But when it came to the trial he changed his mind and pleaded not guilty, so strong was the love of life, even life in prison and without her.

Strong, too, is the natural resistance to these warning signs, and surely up to a point right. To keep going is good advice for a doctor to give the old and I do not suppose that a spiritual adviser would give them very different counsel. He would, however, commend acceptance of old age's limitations as obedience to God's will; and again the doctor's advice would be the same: you must come to terms with your age if you want to keep healthy and happy.

Yet it must, I think, be easier for a Christian to strike a true balance between resisting and accepting what is by ordinary standards a deterioration. Body and mind are running down, or wearing out, but in the old-fashioned language of the Christian the soul is growing all the time in readiness for a new life. And while he will join the humanist (if both are wise) in loving life as it is at every stage in him and in others, life young and strong, life old and unfeebled, he will also welcome that increasing detachment from the world which distinguishes the very old, whether or not they know it or like it. That detachment – I speak as a fool of that part of the haven which I have not yet reached – culminates in the withdrawal of the dying, rooted in physical weakness but not only in that, merciful but not easy for others to accept.

Some die like old Prince Nikolay Bolkonsky, softened by mortal illness out of his pride and cruelty and struggling to ask forgiveness of Marya, the daughter he had loved and ill-treated, before it was too late. But some die like his son, Prince Andrey, turned cold by 'that aloofness from all things earthly' (wrote Tolstoy) 'that is so fearful to a living man' and was so hurtful to that same Marya, the sister he had loved and treated kindly, the sister who had expected that the approach of death would bring kindness, not something like hostility. What she could not understand Tolstoy understood – that with the sense of aloofness from everything earthly he experienced 'a strange and joyous lightness in his being'; that the reason why he seemed not to understand the living was 'not because he had lost the power of understanding but because he understood something else that the living did not and could not understand, and that entirely absorbed him'; that what he understood was that in dying he, a particle of love, was going back to 'the universal and eternal source of love'.

I have not yet experienced much of old age in my own person and so far it is not quite what I expected. There is the

167

fear that suffering and the squalors and embarrassments of senility may come to cloud it, and faith and hope and love all fail before the fashionable lust for longevity allows it to close. The end of it is a frightening but exciting prospect. I still like old age, for what it is and what it promises. I trust that I always shall.

Lady Stocks

Author and broadcaster. Principal of Westfield College, 1939–51.

At the age of eighty-one I find old age distasteful owing to
growing infirmity and diminished mobility. I am a member
of the Euthanasia Society and would like to see the law
changed to enable a doctor to put me out in the event of a
distressing terminal illness or at the moment when I cease to
be a reasoning human being. At present it would be a case
of 'do it yourself' and I only hope adequate means will be
available when the time comes. The compensation of being
eighty-plus is that it provides a good excuse for refusing to
do things that other people ask you to do. In fact I grow
increasingly disinclined for mental or physical exertion of any
sort. It is interesting to see three generations of one's family
growing up, though rather frightening in view of the pressures which the permissive society and the mass media impose on them. Unlike many old people I am not, happily,
threatened by poverty or neglect.

169

Dr Mervyn Stockwood

DD. *Bishop of Southwark, A sermon preached at Great St Mary's, the University Church, Cambridge, 2 November 1969.*

I Corinthians XV, verse 35: 'But some will say, how are the dead raised up? And with what body do they come?'

It was always very interesting planning the services when I was vicar here. 'Life after Death': I was told the undergraduates would not be interested in such a subject. We did it for four Sundays in succession; we only had a queue longer when we had a course on 'Sex'! We had a poll at the university, I remember, – it was pretty representative – and 70% said either they believed in life after death or at any case were prepared to regard it as a possibility. Only 30% ruled it out altogether. I suppose that was about eleven years ago: I don't know how the climate of opinion has changed. But sooner or later a man's thoughts turn towards the grave, and over it is a question mark – Is it the end? It isn't necessarily a question reserved for people who are in the autumn of their life. It is a question which forces itself upon us, sometimes when we are young. I remember a Sunday in May Week when I was talking to undergraduates – friends of mine – and within half an hour of myself talking to them they were dead. Then you are faced with this; or perhaps you undergraduates who have the misfortune to lose your mothers, it seems incredible to you that she who gave birth to you (you who had lived within her for nine months) now a corpse; and the poignancy and grief are almost unendurable. And the question comes: Is it the end?The answer we are likely to give will depend upon our estimate of personality and the body. If we think that personality cannot be dissociated from the body we must assume that life becomes extinct when the brain and heart cease to function. If we see personality as anchored to this body during this life but not identified with it, we may come to a different conclusion. My own conviction is that the evidence is strongly in favour of the latter supposition; that it is anchored, but not identified.

But even if I were not a Christian I should believe in life after death. For many years I have been interested in psychical research. Let me say at once that psychical research has nothing to do with spiritualism as such. It is concerned to study phenomena, not with religious presuppositions.

It may help you to know how I became interested in the subject. It had nothing whatsoever to do with spooks; it was that a friend of mine during the war was staying in the country. There was a house nearby in which no one had lived for some time with a large garden and the owner had said they could pick fruit. My friend went there and because it was so terribly hot she wanted a rest. Someone drew up in a car, got out and she joined them and went into the house. When she told people later, they said: 'You must have been dreaming, nobody lives there, you couldn't get into the house if you wanted to'. She then described what the rooms were like and the colours of the walls. And when they tried to settle it by looking at the house, it was bolted and barred, there was no furniture of any sort, yet my friend had got all the colours in the rooms right and the correct number of rooms! And later it was discovered that the house did belong to a woman with two sons: they were alive at the time, living elsewhere. Now what had happened? Had she entered a pool of memory? I don't know, but it was that which led me to be interested in psychical research and, as I repeat, it had nothing to do with spooks.

The Society for Psychical Research was founded in 1882. It has had several notable presidents including Lord Balfour, Professor Henry Sedgwick and Sir Oliver Lodge. Some have been religious men, others agnostics. The Society has not set out to prove anything, but simply to examine the evidence and to discover whether the facts make it reasonable or unreasonable to believe that there is another world beyond this, and if there is another world to learn something of its nature.

Here are some of the things to which the Society has given its attention: 1. *Clairvoyance*. There are people who allege they see things which are outside time and space as we understand those words. This is what we mean by extra-sensory perception. We establish contact without making use of the customary channels.

2. *Clairaudience*. That's another sort of extra-sensory perception. There are the people who say they hear things and receive messages from another dimension. But not always; it is sometimes from people on this earth. There is not the time to tell you of the numerous claimants that have been examined. Suffice it is to say that in Christian history we need look no further than Joan of Arc and St Paul, both claimed to be clairvoyant and clairaudient. St Paul tells us that on one occasion he was caught up into the next world and he saw and heard things that made such a tremendous impression that he longed to leave this world for the richer and more exciting one he had seen. Again, what about his experience on the Damascus Road when he was converted as a result of a clairvoyant and clairaudient experience? There are those who are afraid of psychical research, who are critical of people like myself who speak about these things. I wonder what they would do if you were to cut out of the Bible all those passages relating to extra sensory perception. Take the story of the transfiguration of Jesus. If that isn't a séance, I don't know what is. There on a top of a mountain Jesus had some sort of psychic experience, his spiritual or etheric body (more about that later) dominated his physical body and he spoke with and saw people who were alleged to be dead, Moses and Elijah. And his friends, who were not normally said to be psychic, themselves both heard and saw much as one does in some seances.

Another matter that the Society for Psychical Research studies is communication – call it thought exchange, call it telepathy, call it what you will between people. Sometimes the people are still alive in this world but living in different places. For instance, a man in Australia and a man in London sit down at a particular moment and write down identical messages. There is also a communication between people who are in this world and those who are in another dimension – the people we speak of as dead. This communication is usually done through a third person who is known as a sensitive, or more commonly, a medium. I have often experienced this sort of communication – I have known what is in a letter before I've opened it – and perhaps one of the most interesting to come before the Society for Psychical Research was shortly after one of its presidents, Mr Myers, had died. Members of the Society went to three mediums in different parts of the world and through them asked Mr Myers, who was dead, to communicate with them in Latin and Greek. Not one of the mediums knew one another. Not one of them could speak Latin or Greek. The message came through in three parts, partly in Latin and partly in Greek, and when put together made a coherent whole. The investigators, all of whom were Cambridge dons, were convinced of the survival of Mr Myers and of his ability to communicate.

Of course a difficulty arises when people depart from scientific standards and resort to anybody, a fortune teller or a medium, who claims to have psychic gifts. What disturbs me about so much alleged psychic phenomena is their sheer banality. I have read a number of sermons that are supposed to come from parsons who, while they were on this earth, were famous for their preaching – Newman, Studdert-Kennedy and Archbishop Temple. (All have preached here in this pulpit). Not one has impressed me. In fact, if they are really true records one can only assume that the transference to the next world hastens mental senility and moral decay, because all these alleged sermons have been the kind of stuff for

173

which a third-rate journalist on a local paper would have got the sack! This leads me to suppose that the alleged sermon either comes from the subconscious and possible fraudulent ramblings of the medium, or from a defective spirit impersonating a famous man. That is a point which I put to you for serious consideration whenever you are considering psychic phenomena. Whatever conditions await us in the next world, it is reasonable to assume that men like Cardinal Newman and Archbishop Temple are usefully employed in the service of God and are not standing in a sort of unemployment queue of variety artists waiting an opportunity to join the Frost Programme. And the possibility that communication with the next world through a medium may bring us into contact not with the person whom we want, but with a foolish earthbound spirit impersonating him is one of the greatest dangers of spiritualism.

I remember that when I was vicar of Great St Mary's I listened to a tape recording of an alleged talk between a member of this congregation and her dead husband. It lasted more than an hour. I can only describe the conversation as drivel. Most of it was taken up with horse racing and there were long descriptions of celestial racing stables and race courses. The woman, quite naturally, was more interested in racing conditions in this world, especially as Derby Day was only three days off. So was I! So she asked what horse was going to win and her husband replied: 'There are so many good entries it would be difficult to say'. It sounded like a quotation from Hansard. Now I don't tell you all this to amuse you but to warn you, because this is territory which demands intellectual integrity and I would say moral perception.

And now let us turn to survival and the nature of the next world. I have made reference to an experience of St Paul. This is what he actually said: 'I heard words that cannot, indeed must not, be translated into human speech. I don't know whether I was in this body or outside it when it happened'. And the implication of this remark is that St Paul was aware of two bodies – the physical and the spiritual. Spiritualists refer to this second body as the etheric body. It is a counterpart body associated with the natural body. Whether or not this is true there are many people who are psychic who claim to see the etheric body. They say it overlaps the natural body. Moreover in certain conditions it would seem that a man's etheric body can be seen by people who are not normally psychic. Moses on Sinai underwent an intense spiritual experience and when he came down to the people his face was shining. Something similar happened to Jesus on the Mount of Transfiguration. There is a fascinating sentence in one of the Gospels. The writer talks about the brilliance of his body and this is exactly what one would expect if the etheric body dominates the physical. It takes some hours to readjust itself, and we are told that when Jesus came down and the people met him, they were afraid. It doesn't say why they were afraid. My guess is that he confronted them much as Moses did and the etheric body was so dominating that even those who were not normally psychic were able to see it. Perhaps both men had been confronted by a spiritual experience so intense that their spiritual, or etheric, body, had so completely dominated their physical body that it was apparent to everybody. Dr W. R. Matthews, until recently the Dean of St Paul's, has given much study to these matters and he says; 'We cannot say much about the spiritual body because we cannot imagine what it would be like to have a body different from that which we now inhabit, but it seems to me reasonable to believe that we are weaving our spiritual bodies as we go along. They are being formed by our thoughts and acts of will and imagination during this life'.

To believe in the physical and etheric bodies seems to be a possible hypothesis, and I think St Paul throws light on the subject when he says: 'At present we are like men looking at a landscape in a small mirror. All we see is a baffling reflection of reality! The time will come when we shall see reality whole and face to face'. By this he means that just as blinkers over the eyes of a horse keeps them fixed on the road so as not to be diverted, so our earthly body is a sort of blinker to help us to keep our minds fixed on the things that belong to our earthly existence. After all while we are here we must give our minds to the job at hand, but not to the exclusion of everything else. An athlete will devote himself to the contest for which he is preparing. He does not forget entirely the larger world in which the contest is set – his family relationships, sending Christmas presents, paying bills, filling in income tax returns. Similarly with our two bodies. The physical body acts as a blinker on the spiritual body. But we need to remember that one day the physical body will dissolve into dust and ashes and the spiritual or etheric body will be freed from its prison house. That is why a wise man trains and disciplines his spiritual body. The more we become slaves to the physical body, the more we are imprisoning the spiritual body and the less conscious of the greater world beyond this one. God in his wisdom has placed over our spiritual bodies, as we pass through this earthly life, a veil which partially obstructs our view of reality. He does this because if there were no veil the things of this world might cease to interest us altogether. And that would be disastrous. At the same time we need to remember that we live our lives in the shadow of eternity. So much then for the resurrection body. It is a spiritual body intermingled with our physical body but freeing itself from the physical body at the moment of death.

What about the nature of the world to which the spiritual body goes? Spiritualists speak of a world in which we eat and drink, listen to music, play games, keep gardens, do most of the things that we do here. And before we insist that this is nonsense we should remember that Jesus himself looked forward to the day when he would feast with his disciples in the next world. How can we make sense of it? The trouble is, we can only think and speak of the next world in the terms of this world. No other language would be meaningful. Suppose it were possible for you to communicate with a

176

baby in the womb of its mother a day or two before birth. Suppose the baby was capable of intelligent conversation. He asks you to tell him what the world outside the womb was like. How would you begin to answer his question? He understands nothing but the conditions inside the womb, and you would be compelled to attempt to explain the conditions of this world in his. That is why it is not surprising that people who are on the other side of the grave use our conditions to illustrate theirs. They can do no other.

My own view is that the normal rules of growth apply. We shall carry on in our new dimension much as we have left off here. As our souls develop fresh possibilities open up to us. We do not pass catastrophically from earth to heaven, from ignorance to infallibility, from imperfection to perfection. Spiritualists tell us that people with strong prejudices and inhibitions only gradually lose them. For example, a narrow-minded sectarian will continue for some time after death to shield himself from any contact with those of another sect, and these inhibitions only give way by degrees as further light is given. Orthodox Christians believe much the same. 'In my Father's house are many resting places'. It does not matter whether we call these resting places Purgatory or Paradise. What matters is that when we die we discard our bodies for good and all, and they return whence they came, earth to earth, ashes to ashes, dust to dust. But we survive as persons. We do not go through a dim shadowy life, wandering aimlessly as ghosts, nor do we become impersonal atoms in some vast unconscious spiritual lump, but we pass to a life full and complete with enhanced powers of expression through our spiritual bodies.

Now let me make my last point which takes us to the heart of the matter. Jesus said: 'I am the Resurrection and the life; he that believeth in me, though he were dead, yet shall he live; and whosoever believeth in me shall never die'. Christian immortality does not begin with physical death. It begins when our beings are united with Christ. What I mean is this – because we are sons of God, made in the divine image, we discover our true selves when our personalities find fellow-ship with the spirit of God, and we begin to be at home not only in this world but in the counterpart spiritual world as well. Sooner or later we must find that atonement, at-one-ment, when our lives are lived on the basis of being at one with the living Christ and with both dimensions of reality. What is the point of survival anyway? I put that to you as forcefully as I can. What is the purpose of survival unless it be in a life of progress to a fuller understanding of God and a closer reunion? I doubt if I should want to survive were it not for that. I remember asking a don at this university when I first came to Great St Mary's if he believed in life after death and he said: 'No'. When I asked him just before I went he said: 'Yes, I now regard it as a regrettable possibility'. And I asked him why it was regrettable and he said, 'My dear Mervyn, the thought of continuing indefinitely with my colleagues at high table fills me with dismay'. And there's a great deal of sense in that. Why go on aimlessly and endlessly? But there is a point and purpose if it means growth in the Spirit and union with God.

Psychic phenomena, interesting though they are, and a proper subject for research for the inquiring mind, do not of themselves lead to spiritual fruition. In fact an excessive interest in table-turning, automatic writing, poltergeists and ectoplasmic materialisation can dim our spiritual sensititivy. What ultimately convinces me of the spiritual world is not a spirit taking hold of a medium at a séance and doing extraordinary things through him, but the Holy Spirit taking hold of a man's life and revealing through him the fruits of love, joy, peace, humility, goodness and self-control.

That is the secret of resurrection; that is the gift of eternal life.

Harold Sutton

(Pseudonym adopted for personal reasons) Ex-teacher. Author, lecturer.

I was born and reared in a thickly-populated area of the Midlands; it was just after the turn of the century and I knew little else but hard living conditions and a great deal of poverty. People seemed to look old before they actually became old. Anyone over the age of forty was old for they wore an old look on their countenance. Deep furrows in their brow; a look of anxiety in their eyes; lean features because of undernourishment and most of the men were bald because of the heat in the pits, in the hot ovens of pottery works and steel furnaces. All this plus a heavy burdensome gait with no spring in their stride gave the impression that 90% of the population were suffering from some oppression. Later in life when I participated in a performance of Handel's great Oratorio, 'Israel in Egypt' and sang the words: 'They oppressed with burdens and made them serve with rigour', my mind always returned to this hard-pressed population within which I grew up from childhood to early manhood. No wonder then that I heard on many occasions some weary person say: 'I wish the Good Lord would take me'.

Since those early days of my life I have taken a keen interest in old people and, from time to time, when I have become sufficiently familiar with an old person who shared my interest in 'things eternal' I have asked: 'What are your thoughts when you contemplate your coming death for you know that at your age, death may come to you at any moment?' The answer has invariably been the same or at least on the same lines: 'Well you know . . . I never think about it. I get on with my daily activities and never give a thought to the subject of dying.' That, I suppose, is very good but it is good only because of the attitude most western people have come to adopt towards death. Death is a natural element of our existence, just as birth is natural, and the occurrence of death should bring the same quality of rejoicing as does the first smile of a newly-born babe. It is beyond me why the passing of a person from this stage of life into the next stage (no matter what existence that is) should be the signal to wear dark clothes, look sad and unhappy and generally take on an attitude of gloom. Of course we miss the loved one; of course we shall feel the vacancy, but are not the sadness, the grief and the weeping an expression of selfishness? I belong to a small group of friends who, when we hear of a death, usually say: 'Thanks be to God, John has gone a step further, he is all right now'. It is all a question of how well we have been educated in the subject of death.

A walk through any geriatric ward will make it obvious that no one is particularly 'looking forward' to the approaching end of life. Geriatric care is a credit to our social system and one could argue that such hospitals are there to give care and attention to the bodies of those who cannot care for themselves. But the right attitude towards their old age would eliminate much of the suffering. Even before a baby is born, the State takes a hand in making sure that the child has every advantage. Pre-natal clinics, like geriatric units, are evidence of social evolution. In education the child again is cared for as never before and great sums of money are spent to make sure that no chance is taken when the child reaches a point of choosing a career. The 1944 Butler Act of Education has provided specialists in every conceivable subject. So it goes on: further education, adult education, grants for this course, grants for that. Nothing is spared. But when does one hear of a week-end course of lectures, meditation, etc. on the subject of death? All the vast sums of money provided for the education and care of people mentioned

180

above are spent on something which may never happen; something which may never be necessary, but the one certain thing in life, the one area where education is vital, the one natural function which requires 'preparation of mind', this is completely neglected except by those few who take it upon themselves to meditate upon those things which are eternal.

Here on earth we are bounded and controlled by the dimension of time. When we die we are excluded from this dimension and we enter (so we are told) a state of being where there is no time. The antithesis of time is eternity and one day someone will dare to announce that it is incumbent upon our administrators to accommodate for education in this subject. If it is important for a child to be prepared for life, (which may end at any minute) it must be equally important for the child and adults also to be educated in that element which is the only certain thing in life, that is, the passing from earth to a state which is non-physical. 'A thousand ages in thy sight is like an evening gone'. Two familiar lines from a hymn could easily provide the basis for a weekend study in the matter of death. Imagine it! No time! It would be useless to try and cram such education into the few years left after a lifetime of activity. People must be educated to accept death with grace and quietude just as a woman accepts her time of difficulty when it is time for her babe to arrive. Death must be looked forward to, anticipated with a degree of keen pleasure. Add this subject to the numerous advertisements on mass media. Make bible reading as common as the daily paper. Or, for that matter, the reading of religious documents from other religions. The Bible is full of spontaneous healings and stories of man's spiritual intercourse with God. But, it would not be necessary for a man or woman to become religious in order to become prepared for death. People prepare for a holiday months ahead, the holiday may never materialise. They prepare for life in education and vocational training, they prepare for everything which may never happen, but they neglect the certainty. In this respect, observe the conduct of animals when they know that death is near. They have natural instincts which man has lost because of his materialistic attitude to life from the moment he can read and write; from the moment he comes under the influence of men of the world. Death is the gateway to the world of spirit, therefore education in spirit is the only suitable preparation for it. Take away the gloom and despair from the scene of death and the despatch of the body; that would be a good first step. Eliminate such hymns as that which contains the words: 'Soon will you and I be lying . . . Each within our narrow bed'. Make death a cheerful thing; a process by which we return to our original home. To the intelligent the subject of predestination may be introduced and attention drawn to the words of Jesus when he warned with such clearness: 'You may be forgiven almost any of your sins . . . except . . . if you harm or hinder one of these little ones. You may as well throw yourself into the sea for you will be damned. For of such *is* the Kingdom of Heaven'.

If people could be made aware that they existed before this life, not only would many questions be answered but people might begin to look forward to their return home. The old hymn 'Heaven is my home' would take on new significance.

A few years ago I met an old man in a wood outside the city of Moscow. We talked for a long time and at last I chanced to ask him: 'What advice would you give to young people about to start their journey through life?' After much thought he said: 'I will answer your question with a Russian proverb. *Konyets Vyenchayet Dyela*. This means: The end crowns the matter. I asked for a full interpretation and he replied: 'It is a state (the condition) of a man's mind at the moment of death which is of prime importance. How far is the man *prepared* for the next existence?' He went on to tell me of his views of the scene of the Crucifixion when the *criminal*, the *malefactor*, the *hardened thief*, rebuked his companion on the third cross: 'Why do you jeer at this man? We deserve this death for we offended against the law; this man has done nothing to deserve death'. My Russian companion explained that he was sure that the malefactor recognised the innocence of Jesus; he also admitted his own guilt and he was forgiven and promised a place in Paradise *that very day*. No waiting in Purgatory. He had qualified, for in a flash he had prepared himself. Hence the Russian proverb: *Konyets vyen-chayet dyela*.

Preparation for death must commence at the age when the Church makes young people aware of their spiritual growth: that is, at about the time of Confirmation. The preparation for the return to spirit must be gradual and pleasant. The same constant, relentless reminder of the pleasantness of death must be maintained in the same way as formal education is rammed into the child until he or she becomes proficient. Until we put the preparation for death on the same basis as the preparation for life we shall always have this sense of mystery and gloom. A person who has died is at peace as far as this world is concerned. The dead person is released from the vulgarity of this world and is free. We are steeped in this world. Let us teach men and women that they originally belonged to another, more beautiful world and that one day they will return there. Stop putting a high price on furniture, pictures, minerals from under the earth, pottery, and so on. Start putting a high price on peace of mind, good conduct and the ability to meet danger and ill-fortune with calmness and quietude. Then will death really lose its sting. I am sure that it was the daily preparation for death which enabled the martyrs to go to the stake and the gibbet without a fear. They knew that they were going to a better place. Educate people on these lines in the most elementary form and we shall see less sad faces in the rooms of old peoples' homes and in the geriatric wards. The casting off of fear which at present accompanies the approach of old age will bring a renewal of health and a brighter outlook of those willing to learn. But the way must be shown to old people, and this can be done only by providing experts in the subject, people specially trained in this field of thought.

Philip Toynbee

Novelist and reviewer.

All we can usefully do is to hand out our interim reports as the years pass, and mount below us. That seems a reasonably apt image now that I have reached my fifty-seventh year: it is as if time passed were some kind of jack, heaving me up another inch or two at every birthday. The view gets better all the time; the air gets fresher; and the only immediate danger comes from looking down too often and falling into the melancholy and irrational dizziness of nostalgia.

I have no doubt whatever that I have been happier, during my fifties, than I was during my laborious progression through any earlier decade. My teens? The usual misery and confusion, lit by the usual dazzling lights. My twenties? A long gluttony for every sort of experience, regardless of all the familiar warnings and quite regardless of the pain I caused to others, the shame to myself. In my early thirties there was a marital disaster – it seemed at the time to be an irremediable catastrophe: tears, rage and exile: the powerful sense that life was already over and that it had totally destroyed me. New marriage and new hope at thirty-four, and from then until fifty a slow settling down: the image of a sediment gradually sinking to the bottom of a glass and leaving the liquid clear. But there was a good deal of physical and mental distress in my middle forties, which I ascribed to some sort of mental and spiritual change-of-life; the unwilling but enforced recognition of middle-age.

But at about the age of fifty recognition of middle-age –

even advanced middle-age – was rewarded by an astonishing regeneration; a kind of happiness and hope which I had never known or thought possible at any earlier point. This was accompanied by – but certainly not caused by – the gentlest and most unpauline form of religious conversion. 'Conversion'? The word is much too dramatic: I had slipped, or blundered, across that invisible frontier which divides what is called unbelief into what is (just) called belief. But much more important than this was a new intensity in the pleasure I took from the ordinary substance of my life. I live deep in the country, surrounded by neighbours who are also close and much-valued friends. At home the three children of my second marriage have scurried, all too quickly, from infancy towards maturity. We do our shopping every week in a little market town for which I feel a passionate affection which I would have denied, until recently, even as a *possible* emotion.

Although I have lived most of my life in the country it is only very recently that I have begun to live the life of the country. (Earlier, except in the pleasures of fishing and gardening, this 'country life' had been simply the retreat of someone who is incapable of living in cities without self-destruction.) During the last year I have become a bicyclist, ecclesiologist, an amateur builder, a photographer, a home-brewer: now I have further plans for a sustained (observational) assault on the flora and fauna. It is, I suppose, a form of private conservatism, sharply endorsed and intensified by my belief that our technological civilisation is doomed whether it knows this or not (But I remain an integral egalitarian in politics, and I seldom forget for long that I owe much of my present happiness both to the good fortune of a good fortune and to a congenial job which allows me to live where I wish and to work according to my own routine).

Meanwhile I have been writing a long book for the past twenty years, and I mean to go on doing so for at least another five. If all goes well another long book awaits me after that. It is strange – at least it interests *me* – that I should have left it so late to mention my 'life work'. I think the reason must be that, although I respect this literary monster, and could not live happily except in the company of him or another of his kind, yet I have never been able to take 'Art' altogether seriously. I write verse, and I believe that much of it is very good verse, but I can never regard myself as 'a poet'. Nor is it any longer of much interest to me whether my work will 'live' or not; it serves its own purpose, now, in the writing of it: I hope it will give some illumination to others; but it looks more and more like bread cast on the waters, and a kind of bread which has not yet proved very appetising either to the fish or to the seagulls.

But there is a flaw in all this complacency – which is that my fear of death remains almost undiminished. It was keen and constant in childhood; hardly a day, never a week, of adult life has passed without a *momento mori*. *Timor mortis conturbat me*. Why? Certainly not because I fear what lies on the other side of death: my belief in total extinction is almost total, and whenever it wavers I feel nothing but a nervous joy at the idea that survival might be conceivable after all. No; it is obliteration itself which fills me with a literally unspeakable horror: and the more I enjoy my life the longer – reasonably enough – I want it to go on (Almost every day I count the diminishing years between me, my present age and a fabulous century).

And yet I also know that there is a reason beyond this ordinary, earthly reason. I know that those who have been *really* happy on earth – I am thinking of the happiness which accompanies goodness – have not dreaded death in the least. And this has been equally true of the believing and the disbelieving saints. This higher happiness springs, of course, from a conquest of self which I haven't even begun to achieve. It springs from a total indifference to possessions: I love my possessions and am constantly buying new ones. It springs from a turning outwards towards the world not in order to make demands on it but in order to live within its own laws and discovered harmonies. I am turned outwards,

186

for the most part, but still with a sort of greed and longing. I want to *possess* that sky, this swollen river; all these loved faces (And if I say that I want to possess them in order to transform them into my own work this is true but not very relevant: the greed is wrong, whatever we mean to do with our acquisitions).

Finally, of course, there is old age itself, hurrying towards me; scarcely two decades away by now (and when I look two decades *back* it seems like yesterday.) The plight of the aged! Recently the BBC has rubbed our noses in it, and very properly. Since I am fairly well off, since I have affectionate children who will not immure me in even the 'nicest' of homes, since I have a wife who is younger than I am and famous for her unforced love and goodness, it is unlikely that I shall suffer the worst pains and ignominies of old age. But if I live to be very old – and this is what I mean to do – it is almost certain that my body will collapse before my will to live collapses. I shall be incontinent; arthritic; forgetful; crotchety – perhaps a nuisance to others and a burden to myself. The only hope here – for every one of us – is that we can somehow attain the serenity of total acceptance before what we have to accept becomes intolerable to any lesser state of mind than that.

Today my body is still in very good order. Mercifully my sexual appetite has abated: appetite and opportunity have trotted downhill together in amicable harness (I *in no way* regret the declension of my genitals – though like all men I often wish that in my time I had had all the women in the world). But I can still run or bicycle a long way: I still enjoy long hours of manual work; eating is a greater pleasure than ever, particularly on those alternate days when I revert to my old carnivorous habits. The fact is, I suppose, that in every worldly sense I am a very happy man, but that I have not yet discovered how to be happy in any other sense (Yet even in this continued failure I feel that I may be a little nearer to success than I have ever been before).

Sir George Trevelyan

Bart. MA. Warden of Altringham Park, the Shropshire Adult College, from 1947 to his retirement in 1971, when he founded the Wrekin Trust for promoting conferences on approaches to spiritual knowledge.

So you are retiring? You are facing the advance of old age, and with it the prospect of death. Splendid. This is a great stage to have reached. But it is immensely important to discuss our attitude towards these great things of life.

It is strange to think that ours is the only period in world history in which virtually the whole of society is given a dozen free years after the career is finished or the family launched. Previously life consisted basically of nurture, training and toil until worn out. Now, through medical advance and the social services, death is postponed and like a free gift we each have this spell of time in which to harvest the life experience we have made. Now we can leave the arena and go at a gentler pace.

It is interesting that many enter retirement with anxiety. Sometimes the transition is just too sudden. A business executive who has held great responsibility and has had a routine of office life may feel as if something has snapped. The bottom seems to fall out of life. Apparently there are many who break down and even die after a couple of years of retirement. Many simply take on some other form of work so as to feel fully employed.

Basically, we should accept that this is a new phase in life, a culminating experience. It is not just that our energies are less than they were and that we must rest more. It is a period with a purpose of deep significance.

Our lives fall into seven-year periods. At seven we grow

our wisdom teeth, at fourteen reach puberty, at twenty-one come of age, at twenty-eight are at the top of our strength, at forty-two often take on the greatest responsibility, but at sixty-three we reach what is called the 'climacteric'. We move into the time leading to the august stage of 'three score years and ten'. Recognise this change at about sixty-three as an entry into a real new soul-period, in which we can begin to work on ourselves in a new way.

We withdraw from the activity of the arena of life. With the relaxing of the pressures of a career our activities should now take on a different emphasis. It is not by any means that we need to become idle, but rather that the emphasis must turn inward more, towards a deeper development.

T. S. Eliot put it well in 'East Coker':

> Old men ought to be explorers.
> Here and there does not matter
> We must be still, and still moving
> Into another intensity,
> For a further union, a deeper communion . . .
> In my end is my beginning.

What do these enigmatic lines really mean?

Our whole attitude towards retirement and old age is conditioned, positively or negatively, by our beliefs about the meaning and purpose of life – and death. Let me summarise the world-view which is emerging so rapidly in many minds in our time. Through our materialistic culture a fine new wind is blowing which fills many people with the certainty that life is about something quite different from mere 'getting and spending'. A spiritual world-view is beginning to colour our thinking. A materialistic outlook is primarily one of outward looking – a concern with things and the acquiring of more of them, desires and their satisfaction. This of course is important but there is an inward exploration also possible. William Blake, that great seer of the New Age, wrote: 'I cease not from my great task, to open the Eternal Worlds, to open the Immortal Eye of Man, inwards, into the Worlds of Thought, into Eternity, ever expanding in the Bosom of God, the Human Imagination'.

By looking inward in the right way we can learn to look through and out into realms undreamt of in our ordinary life. Then we discover that Life is something which can never be destroyed. It is eternal and it is a great oneness. There is a kernel in each of us which is imperishable. The body may break down and be destroyed but the core of a man, the real individuality, is a spiritual entity which is beyond death. If this be so then it is the most important piece of knowledge we can get, particularly in a culture which tacitly assumes that death is the end and that 'we' are extinguished with the destruction of brain and sense mechanism. This is no new knowledge. In our culture we have simply forgotten it or lost the means of making it real and meaningful to ourselves. All the great cultures of the past have, broadly speaking, recognised that the core of a man is a droplet of the Divine Source and as such is imperishable.

Now in an age of anxiety and doubt, of agnosticism and cynicism, of materialism and rivalry, of atheism and indifference to the spirit, there re-emerges the ageless wisdom in a form which our modern intellects can take. And with it comes a flood of joy and re-assurance, awakening a great hope for man's future even in this time when doom-laden prophecies seem to hang over a society in which death and catastrophe play so large a part. For if the 'soul' is eternal there can be no death in the sense of extinction. The worn-out sheath of the body will be discarded and the liberated soul will move back to the plane from which it descended and to which it truly belongs. We begin to see that the soul is on a long allegorical journey descending from realms of light into the darkness and density of matter in order to learn lessons through its trials and ordeals that it may then rise further towards the Divinity of which it is a part.

Thus we grasp clearly that *we are not our bodies*. We, the real 'we', the imperishable spiritual core, takes to itself a body as a necessary sheath so that it may live in the world of substance. We live *through* our bodies, which develop and age and must be discarded in due time. Our birth is a descent into drastic limitation. It is like a descent into a kind of tomb. Death then is a release from limitation into the wider consciousness which is the soul's true home. It is more like a birth.

The important thought is that we were there as a developed entity before we were born. *Pre-existence* is a concept which must be conceived. There is much speculation about survival after death. If we can accept the postulate of the imperishable entity, then survival is axiomatic. The droplet of life cannot be extinguished. Of course we survive. It need hardly be discussed. But to get clear on the concept of pre-existence is important, for it gives us a new humility and sense of responsibility. We see that there is a long spiritual evolution for the soul. Before entering birth we were extended in consciousness in the planes of light.

Wordsworth saw this; think again those well known lines in 'The Intimations of Immortality in Early Childhood':

Our birth is but a sleep and a forgetting:
The soul that rises with us, our life's star,
Hath had elsewhere its setting,
And cometh from afar;
Not in entire forgetfulness,
And not in utter nakedness,
But trailing clouds of glory do we come
From God, who is our home.
Heaven lies about us in our infancy;
Shades of the prison-house begin to close
Upon the growing boy,
But he beholds the light, and whence it flows,
He sees it in his joy;
The youth, who daily farther from the east
Must travel, still is Nature's priest,
And by the vision splendid

Is on his way attended;
At length the man perceives it die away,
And fade into the light of common day.

As he aged, Wordsworth lost the earlier vision.

In our time the task for the senior citizen is to reawaken the 'vision splendid' and advance towards the ultimate release with ever mounting anticipation, hope and joy.

When you see a wee child, don't say: 'Look at that tiny little soul'. It may be a great and developed soul beginning to enter into a tiny puling frame. It will take its twenty-one years fully to incarnate, to come of age.

When you see an old man, don't say: 'Look at that poor old soul'. It is an ageless soul suffering the limitations of an ageing body. The soul is a thing of eternal youth moving between expansion on the higher planes and experience of limitation within a body. Thus the last years should be a progressive release from identification with the body, just as the first years were a progressive entry.

You see how this spiritual world-view must colour our attitude to our years of retirement and ageing. The soul is being prepared for a great release. At the height of its physical powers and in the full glory of its senses it has closely identified itself with substance. Now with the body's power failing it should turn, not with reluctance but with the joy of understanding, towards the great task of preparation for its release.

The task of man on earth is to build his permanent spiritual individuality. For this we are here. We carry with us into the life beyond only that which we have spiritualised of our faculties and thinking. That which is solely concerned with mundane affairs will fade. Alas, that so many who have not realised that consciousness goes on, make no preparation whatever. It is as if they were to enter a higher university without even taking one O-level examination.

For those whose minds are open and flexible there is now an overwhelming body of evidence to prove survival and

192

pre-existence. The critical intellect may always try to debunk and disbelieve. We now recognise that the mind can apprehend truth directly and does not need 'scientific' proof in a field where weighing and measuring are impossible. There is no space in this essay to go deeply into the picture of the life beyond given us through communication and communion with those who have passed on. Be it said here that there is no attempt in what I have written to enforce belief. Rather is this an invitation to *think*. If the outlook attracts you, think it; hold it as a view of life and if it is true it will attract other thoughts, and strengthen you in your whole attitude of courage in facing 'the future'.

A new quality of communion with our friends on the higher planes is now becoming possible. Remarkable truths were found by trance mediums of integrity. Now more and more sensitives are finding it possible in fullest consciousness to commune with 'departed' friends. The messages bring a certainty that we are very close to those we love, for we are on the same telepathic wave length. Rather than appearing before us they can speak within our thinking, blending with our own consciousness. Thus we shall appear to give ourselves the answer to our own questions which we send up to them. It is a marvellously intimate form of communion, far subtler than bodily contact. The soul which has moved on is in a subtler body. The communications show that we remain very much ourselves but in a surrounding shaped much more easily by our thought and imagination, since we are freed from the restrictions of dense matter.

The very word 'death' is loaded with the sense of finality and the horror of the rotting cadaver. There is no word in our language to connote the splendour of the release of the soul from the restricting body, an expansion into light.

Thus the new understanding will alter our whole attitude to ageing. Of course the body develops its pains and troubles. We must see it in proportion. What is ten or fifteen years out of eternity? The soul is beginning to free itself from a body which has served its turn. This can be uncomfortable, but there should be ample compensation as the mind and soul attain to a deeper tranquillity and joy in recognising the true goal. The only tragedy is when a person gets enclosed within the aches and pains and fails to gain the 'vision splendid'.

We are not, in our closing years, simply putting time by until we 'rest in the grave'. We are called on to prepare for a great step forward, opening possibilities of wider exploration and holding fascinating prospects. We shall be reunited with those we love. We shall have the opportunity for a full and creative life on a different and wider plane of consciousness, and yet it is clear that essentially we still remain surprisingly ourselves.

One can envisage a new kind of nursing home receiving those who are soon to pass on, but helping them to face the light-filled Gates of Death with joy and courage. We should go through in conscious joy and with the conviction that we shall be received by friends in a world of light. The closing months of life could be something of a ritual preparation, so that the mind can understand what is happening.

We have to feel that as senior citizens we are in a true sense beginning to build a new form of society. There will, obviously, be infinitely varied interests for individuals to follow. What matters is that *some* part of the day is given over to the development of the inner life, in meditation, study of books on the spiritual path, or creative activities. All this clearly will vary according to the soul development of the person concerned. It is the attitude of mind that matters, in recognising that this is a preparatory period rather than a winding up of a life. You can still build faculties and skills which will carry over into the wide reaches of the beyond. You can lift thinking on to a subtler level, less concerned with the world of the senses. Indeed you can develop the subtler inner senses which link you with the 'supersensible' worlds.

Yeats, in his poem 'Sailing to Byzantium', gives us a grand image of ageing:

An aged man is but a paltry thing,
A tattered coat upon a stick, unless
Soul clap its hands and sing, and louder sing,
For every tatter in its mortal dress,
Nor is there singing school but studying
Monuments of its own magnificence;
And therefore have I sailed the seas and come
To the holy city of Byzantium!

To Yeats Byzantium was not only a beautiful city but sym-
bolised a higher state of consciousness. We are truly concerned with adult education to which there is literally no end.

From the concept of the eternal nature of the soul and the
infinite importance of life on earth as a training ground, it
logically follows that we must have visited this earth many
times. Otherwise, soul evolution would seem impossible.
One life is clearly not long enough for much development.
Thus the postulate of re-incarnation makes sense to many
people and restores meaning to life. There is no obligation
to accept it, but if we learn to live with it as a thought its
probable truth is born in upon us.

Recognise that life in a body is a drastic limitation of the
soul. We take over a body and learn to work with it. It is the
necessary implement for a free-ranging spirit to be slowed
down in vibratory rate and so to act effectively in the material
plane. The senses really should be seen as filters which allow
only a little of the splendour of the cosmos into our consciousness. Here is another short poem by Martin Armstrong
which he calls 'The Cage':

Man, afraid to be alive
Shuts his soul in senses five
From fields of uncreated light
Into the crystal tower of sight,
And from the roaring songs of space
Into the small flesh-carven place
Of the ear whose cave impounds

Only small and broken sounds,
And to his narrow sense of touch
From strength that held the stars in clutch,
And from the warm ambrosial spice
Of flowers and fruits of paradise,
Into the frail and fitful power
Of scent and tasting, sweet and sour;
And toiling for a sordid wage
There in his self-created cage
Ah, how safely barred is he
From menace of Eternity.

The essence of earth-life is not only limitation but loss. We must learn to forgo. Our lives of course are filled with the experience of loss, disappointments, sacrifice of hopes. But now know that on the higher plane we shall find again those we have loved and lost. The loss is all a training of the soul. Do you remember Samuel Butler's delightful *misquotation* – 'It is better to have loved and lost than never to have *lost* at all'! Furthermore on the higher planes it appears that we get the opportunity to fulfil the things we had hoped to do and achieve. Frustration on earth can lead to fulfilment in higher worlds. Our task here is to accept the loss and transmute the unfulfilled longing into aspiration. By the loss we learn where our real love lies and can set the heart to aspiration and anticipation of fulfilment on another level. 'All which thy child's mistake fancies as lost I have stored for thee at home: Rise, clasp My hand and come!' So speaks the Christ Being in Frances Thompson's 'Hound of Heaven'.

Yet now at the close of this essay let us recognise that all this is not simply a selfish desire for the 'saving of our soul'. Old age has a function in the very redemption of mankind. We live in an age of spiritual awakening. A New Age is coming in which the power of the spirit becomes apparent working through every aspect of life. The veils between the planes of consciousness are thinning. A new society begins to form, fired by a new ardour and a love which transcends the personal and unites with the Divinity in all things. The younger generation, very many of them, sense what is happening. Hence their 'rebellion' in quest of new ways to widen consciousness. They know that great changes must come and that much that works on the old laws must be swept away, but that the New is filled with the Living Spirit. There never was such an Age to be alive. But we know there is no death. We are always 'alive' on this plane or that. If we are old we are not 'out of the game'. In spirit we are eternally young. It matters little whether we are working from earth bodies or on the higher spheres. The river of death turns out to be a trickle and we shall still be in touch when we have gone over. Thus those of us who are shortly to be released from ageing bodies may still take part in the great changes. By understanding the stupendous spiritual picture of the birth of a New Age, the Age of Aquarius and of the Holy Spirit, the older people are helping to lift the whole body of consciousness towards the light. Go forward into the light with joy that we are all involved. Discover the timeless ageless being within you and rejoice. 'Not farewell, but fare forward, voyagers'.

Margaret Trouncer

Author. Awarded New York Catholic Literary Foundation Prize.

I love impending old age very much because each day draws one nearer to God, to leaping into the light. I'm told that even the suffering souls in Purgatory are happy. So why be afraid? God knows how much we can bear, and will never try us beyond our strength. And he'll always give grace. Let us pray to St Joseph, patron of a happy death!

I am not afraid of death. I can't understand the people who are, but I have very definite views about how the old can help themselves. Was it not the poet, Virgil, who still wrote when he was a hundred years old, or am I wrong? One of my best friends was the Master of the Garth Hunt and he was still hunting at eighty-four, drinking vintage port and driving ferociously around the lanes of Berkshire with me in a dogcart. I think it's such a mistake to curtail all activities with the excuse, 'Oh, I'm getting on, you know'. That is no excuse at all.

May I speak a moment about the health point of view; rheumatism being the terrible British enemy of the old. I wish they would not resign themselves to its miseries so easily. So much can be done, for instance, by the Charterhouse Rheumatism Clinic in London. Then, I am a great believer in health foods, though one shouldn't become a crank, of course. The great Olaf Amundsen, the nephew of the polar explorer, cured frightful stomach trouble by eating small quantities of grated raw vegetables, and he told me himself that vegetables are so ill-treated now with insecticides that they should be scrubbed before use. The other great temptation for the old is not to eat at all because they can't be bothered. Very undisciplined I call it. They should make it a positive duty to have one decent, sound meal a day and to give up endless cups of tea and buns, and if they simply cannot manage their own means speak to their doctor about 'Meals on Wheels'. Many old women who have been beautiful all their young days imagine that advancing years deprive them of their good looks. On the contrary, I have met so many charming-looking women with very sweet expressions on their faces, in spite of wrinkles. I don't believe in hair dye or rouge, but I do believe in the utmost cleanliness for the aged, and trying to look as nice as they can manage.

A nurse has just given me the advice that I should not allow people to help me on and off buses just yet, because one gets into the habit of expecting it. Everybody should be independent for as long as possible, and certainly a good brisk walk for half an hour every day in the fresh air is beneficial. If they have a garden then, of course, that helps you through till the end. If they haven't, well they should have window boxes. Flowers have a very therapeutic influence on the aged . . . One of the greatest pleasures of old age is having grandchildren. I can't think why one loves them, even more than one's own children, but my three happen to be particularly delicious children.

The late Dr Harry Walden

Written at the age of 82, contributed by his daughter, Mrs Mary Agace.

Aged far beyond the usual span of years
it matters less *when* I shall die than how,
The act is sure, but not the circumstance
which gives no choice of time or place
except when the desperate or the brave
find life worthless; making their end
when dying seems easier than to live!
How shall I avoid my exit as a Terminal,
cribbed and clinical in growing vacancy?
Dreaming of beyond and its re-unions
from this world to the next – if next there be.
No – Let my end be of the moment. As the
flash of summer lightning splits the tree
which shelters me – a stopped heartbeat, unready
in some quiet happiness, sleep, or noonday nod, ·
There seems no better way for me to die!
Or will some last serenity be granted
to my yielding spirit? Perhaps at the brink
held back briefly by those who love me,
Willing the inevitable moment to wait.—
Shall I outline the many friends I made
who helped to form the pattern of my life
and whom the gathering years make scarcer?
Time is now of lesser consequence to me
than the happiness I remember in recall
when life was sweet. Now moving to its close

shall I be left when none will seek, or care
that the final option left me is to wait
and cloak my loneliness with dignity?

Dom Alberic Stacpoole

OSB, MC, MA, monk of Ampleforth. Soldier, Church historian, editor, schoolmaster.

I write these lines on the evening the news broke that 'God's candidate', Pope John-Paul I, had been taken by God after such a vastly promising pontificate of just thirty-three days. Man proposes, but God disposes: 'This night wilt thou be in paradise with me'. What a mystery it is, and at the heart of man's meeting with God in his Church.

I am not old, but in my middle forties. I am not unacquainted with death, however. As a boy I found myself in the Quetta earthquake, where our houses collapsed and many hundreds died. In the war I found myself in the heavy Belfast raids, which wrecked whole streets near our house. In Korea I found myself engaged in the last full-scale battle that the British Army was asked to fight, watching streams of casualties come off the hill (Hook Ridge) day after day – till I went too. Parachuting, I have been involved in drops where 'chutes did not open, and I was at Port Said in November, 1956. In Africa, I have encountered death by drowning on exercises. Then I exchanged the call of arms for the call of Benedictine Pax.

Those deaths, and others by road accident I was concerned in, were all violent and virtually all of young men and women cut off in their prime. Now in a monastery, an extended family, I began to be involved in the deaths of the old, sometimes the very old – for people ripen in monasteries, waxing strong in the ascetic rhythm of conventual duties, remaining long buoyed up by the impetus of habit as they run down the grooves of prayerful routine. Strange it was to cease living among the young, the lean and the powerful, those who had granted their calling the 'ultimate sanction' of a possible violent death; and to start living among those who died in God's good time, full of grey hairs and an elder's wisdom.

What is in common? Dedication, surrender to the hand of God, either by 'act of God' or the course of God's nature; fearlessness of death as being the most honourable estate, or the state to which all human existence is ordered. Blessed are the dead, for their name liveth for evermore: these dead are blessed, for their spirit has gone to God who made them. Soldiers die, let it be known, for love of peace and for love of principle. Monks die, it need not be said, for love of God and in the hope of sharing the beatific vision. For each, it is the ultimate surrender, and yet the ultimate self-realisation in their calling: both are absolutely what they should be in their act of dying. *Consummatum est.*

What distinguishes them? Youth and age, of course: the difference between the green sapling felled and the old oak falling. The soldier, dying in his calling, never experiences diminishment. There is a prolonged and massive surrender that he need never make, that of growing into decrepitude and senility. He never quite loses the gleam in his eye, nor the juice in his vein, nor the light in his intellect, nor the sharpness of his blade. His standards never need be compromised, nor his values progressively eroded by 'time which trieth all things'. He will know what it is to grieve, but not so frequently nor to the depth of his soul: for the loneliness that comes from progressive desertion by fond friends to another life is seldom his, except in protracted war (I am thinking of the air casualties during 1940–45). He will not see inroads made into the purity of mutual friendship by the dimming of passion, nor the onset of self-absorption, the destructiveness of once-contained vice and the loss of that perspective and humour which is fuelled by the energy of generosity. Nor will he experience the *élan vitale* of those he

counts most dear giving place to a mean husbanding of ebbing resources, or feel the fear of it all in his own bones. But
the poet does not see it all so darkly, nor envy youth its early
surrender:

These laid the world away; poured out the red
Sweet wine of youth, gave up the years to be
Of work and joy, and that unhoped for serene,
That men call age.

'Youth is a blunder', wrote Disraeli in *Coningsby*, 'manhood a struggle, old age a regret'. Surely, for all the rewards
of life well lived, there must always be the resentment that
accompanies failing powers, the apprehension issuing from
our internal diminishment – which may form the darkest
element, the most despairingly useless years of our existence.
When our struggle is slackened to regret, our natural failings
(physical and moral) combine with the failings of our life-
journey (accidents and illnesses, or personal conflicts) to un-
dermine the light and strength and joy by which we presume
to live. Death is the final diminishment, for it spells physical
and moral corruption – and it may not come too soon for
that corruption to wreak its souring effect around us. The
poet warns us of the dangers;

Yet each man kills the thing he loves.
By each let this be heard.
Some do it with a bitter look,
Some with a flattering word. . .
Some kill their love when they are young,
And some when they are old;
Some strangle with the hands of Lust,
Some with the hands of Gold.

To all this, there is only one answer: we must come to
accept our.diminishments for what they are, transfiguring
them in Christ, who foretold: 'In the world you will have

affliction; but take courage, I have overcome the world'. We are asked by the human condition to relive in ourselves the drama of Christ's utter *kenosis*, his self-emptying even unto death in total humiliation, that being the drama of his return to his Father in heaven. We are all called – at every stage of our lives – to enter into Christ's sacrificial surrender, becoming one with the suffering Servant-Saviour if we are ever to become one with him in his glory. This is the meaning of that priceless gift, human existence *in via*. Dying is the breakthrough, not the dissolution: the end is the beginning, pilgrimage becoming paradise for those who have persevered.

It is a most disturbing mystery of our being, trying to reconcile the creative grace of God's goodness with our progressive failure. We should look for the divine synthesis not in our own brief lives nor in the fleeting history of our time, but in a far longer vision. Dare we acknowledge it, we are as soldiers falling in the assault which culminates in peace, our individual defeats composing the corporate victory. We should recall from another age that the blood of the martyrs proved the seed of the Church. Of necessity, there will be ill (sin and evil), for a world purged of it would be a world already in consummation: whereas in fact it is a world in the throes of growth, undergoing the shocks of transfiguration, men being tempered by the ordeal of diminishment or downfall (so it seems), in fact being changed as the pruning knife changes a plant. Coming to die wonderfully concentrates the spirit, detaching us from here and attaching us to Him. It is the steady growth from the bondage of self to the liberation of service of our Sovereign. It is a migration, involving endless little mourning griefs, even desolation brought on by the tearing up of roots and the sadness of fond farewells. Going out to meet our destiny involves going out of ourselves. To be incorporated into Christ and to share in the life of the Trinity means first that we must make space in our own being for that end. As Père Teilhard prayed: 'In these dark moments, O God, grant that I may perceive that it is you painfully parting the fibres of my being to penetrate the

205

marrow of my substance to bear me away with you. Teach me to treat my very death as an act of communion'.

For death, that point where all our possibilities, fully extended and straining for perfection, find themselves overwhelmed; that point, the point of maximal fidelity to the task of human existence, is the point of highest communion with God in resignation. 'Into thy hands I commend my spirit!'

Epilogue

Ralph Ricketts

An aged man is but a paltry thing,
A tattered coat upon a stick, unless
Soul clap its hands and sing, and louder sing
For every tatter in its mortal dress.

W. B. Yeats

Gwendolen Plunket Greene wrote of her uncle, Baron Friedrich von Hügel that, during the last few months of his life, 'he seemed full of a deep peace and content'. I am about the same age as von Hügel was when these words were written but, alas, my condition is very unlike his. Seldom am I peaceful and content for any length of time. My acceptance of old age is intermittent and incomplete. A voice within me still whispers that old age is an illness from which, like any other illness, I shall recover. When, after a good night, I awake refreshed, this childish voice exclaims: 'What did I say? You are better. In a few days you will be well'.

The fact is, I am torn in two. One half of me is still wedded to this world, its loves, activities, delights. Allure persists though capacity weakens. The other half craves a union to which it will never attain in this life ('Only you can give what I long to receive, only you can receive what I long to give'). Perhaps this dichotomy is inevitable, part of our double nature: we are designed to inhabit two worlds at once – hence the tension and the conflict which abate and revive like the anger of the sea. Meanwhile, I glance with distaste at my reflection in the glass; I fumble with the car key; I drop my change in shops; I can't work for as long as I used to be able to; I can no longer play tennis; I can only play nine holes of golf; I can't dance – at least I can but I must look pretty silly when I do. I find all this exasperating, humiliating and embarrassing. The occupations recommended as suitable for my age leave me cold. I can't play chess; I am bored by cards, croquet and bowls; I dislike reminiscing. Nor is the attitude of the young always helpful. Not that they are impatient or unkind, they could not be more patient or kinder. But they seem to take for granted that I am old and will get older. Never, by word or look, do they indicate: 'What is this awful thing that has happened to you? How terrible! I'm sure you never used to be like this'. In my less attractive moods I feel inclined to mutter: 'You wait! It will be your turn next!' And then I remember that, thirty, even twenty years ago, old age was unimaginable to me. If an old man had tried to describe it I would not have believed him; I would have thought he was exaggerating or in the grip of self-pity. No, on the material level there is nothing to be said for old age, or death. Old age is a degradation, death an outrage. The fact that both are natural makes them no more tolerable (Not if you are Henry James, of course, who met his first stroke with: 'So here it comes – the distinguished thing' – *The Lyttelton Hart-Davis Letters*. Edited by Sir Rupert Hart-Davis; John Murray, London).

But if you look at it in a different way the landscape alters dramatically, like a lake on an overcast day when the sun shines suddenly from between the clouds, or a darkened room when the light is switched on. Old age becomes something to be accepted, used, like any other form of pain or discomfort. Death becomes not the end but the beginning. The trouble is, that the sun recedes again behind the clouds, the light in the room is switched off. But the memory of the transformation *can* remain, develop into an ideal by which one may choose to try to live. Old age and death shed their menace, become gentle guests, to be welcomed, if not with an embrace, at least with a friendly handshake. In many ways I am fortunate. I can walk several miles, I can see and hear well, I can swim, I enjoy conversation as much as ever (I must try not to be a bore!).

Old age, I find, is a progress towards aloneness. Not that people, in particular my family and friends, mean less to me; very much the reverse. There is no question for me of 'all passion spent' – I rather wish there were, it would make growing old simpler. But I feel like an onion whose skins are being peeled off one by one so that eventually, stripped of adhesions, the essential core will appear naked and one hopes, eternal. Each man to his own grave; then the Communion of Saints, 'that shining mystery of human solidarity' which, we are informed, includes all men of good will, not only the official saints – otherwise, I should be sadly out of my income-bracket.

I see little point in thinking much about death, still less in trying to imagine what the act of dying and its aftermath will be like. We have not the equipment for such an exercise. We must try to be like children who do not worry about tomorrow. But I remember an occasion when I was considered to be dying. The sensation was delicious – like drifting gently out on a calm sea. I did not want to be revived, to 'come back'. Abbot Chapman writes: 'Usually when people come to die, they are either unconscious, or else quite peaceful, feeling it perfectly natural to die. But when we are *well*, it is naturally repugnant to us' (*The Spiritual Letters of Don John Chapman*, OSB – Sheed & Ward, London).

The old have their face to the wall. There is nothing, in the ordinary sense, for them to look forward to. They may become bored, depressed. Life without purpose is dreary. The ambitions proper to youth and middle age are unseemly in the old. But I believe there is one ambition left: to try and increase my love, knowledge, understanding of God and of other people. This ambition should last me to the end of my life. At the end, I would like to have the faith and courage to be able to say with von Hügel: 'I wait for the breath of God, for God's breath'.

Books of general Christian interest as well as books on theology, scripture, spirituality and mysticism are available from the publishers Burns and Oates and Search Press Limited. A catalogue will be sent free on request. Please apply to:

Burns and Oates/Search Press Limited,
2–10 Jerdan Place, London SW6 5PT
Tel.: 01-385 6261/2